Anonymous World Classic Literature Series

MY

IMMORTAL

A HARRY POTTER FANFIC

THE DEFINITIVE COLLECTION

An annotated edition.

by

Tara Gilesbie

aka. goffikgurl666

aka. XXXmidnitegoffXXX

aka. XXXbloodyrists666XXX

with

Xanthan Gum and **Obvious Troll**

With 2 Extra Stories by

Bloodytearz666

Table of contents

Preface iv

My Immortal vi

My Immortal 2: Wake Me Up Inside cxviii

My Immortal 2: Fangz 4 De Venom clv

A Vampre Wil Nevr Hurt You ccxv

Bonus Story 1. I'm Not Okay ccxlviii

Bonus Story 2. Ghost of You ccli

Character illustartion: Ebony Dark'ness Dementia Raven Way cclxv

"My Immortal" character relationship chart cclxvi

Preface

To say that *My Immortal* has a "plot" might be something of an overstatement. It's more like a loose collection of bad ideas and misspelled words centered around overly long passages about the author's fashion sense and favorite bands. The story is set in some weird, dystopian version of the Harry Potter universe where the struggle between good and evil has been replaced with an eternal struggle between "goths" and "preps," and every main character is either gothic, emo, bisexual, a satanist, a vampire, or any combination of these. The story follows the protagonist **Ebony Dark'ness Dementia Raven Way**, a 7th year student at Hogwarts who wanders around having random sex with HP emo clones and then describes her outfit for several paragraphs. That's seriously about it. There are many other things that happen in the story, but none of it follows any logical progression, so recounting it here would be a pointless endeavor. The story is written in first-person through Ebony's perspective, since Gilesbie couldn't even bother to *pretend* that she wasn't writing her own personal self-insertion fantasy Mary-Sue bullshit.

The plot of *My Immortal* has an astounding number of problems, the least of these being that normal, muggle bands are allowed to have frequent concerts in an all-wizard village, that the story doesn't attempt to follow any laws of physics, or that multiple passages in the story are repeated verbatim. Here's a short checklist of mistakes fanfiction authors often make when writing. Let's see if *My Immortal* commits any of them.

1. **Spelling/Grammar/Usage Errors:** Fun fact: *My Immortal* actually has fewer correctly spelled words than it has chapters.

2. **Canon Rape:** Are you fucking kidding? *My Immortal* rewrote the book on canon rape. You wouldn't even know this was a Harry Potter fanfic if somebody didn't tell you beforehand.

3. **OOC Characters:** Stands for "Out of Character." A few quick examples -

Harry is now a bisexual goth vampire with a pentagram scar, Hermione's name is now B'loody Mary Smith, and Hedwig is no longer a pet owl, but Voldemort's bisexual ex-lover.

4. **Unnecessary/Poorly Written Sex Scenes:** *"Draco climbed on top of me and we started to make out keenly against a tree. He took of my top and I took of his clothes. I even took of my bra. Then he put his thingie into my you-know-what and we did it for the first time."*

5. **Overabundant Pop-Culture References:** Whereas most fanfic authors work their stupid pop-culture references in subtly, Tara takes the opposite approach and actually *centers* her story around her favorite bands and fashion, and occasionally throws in something about the Harry Potter series.

6. **Unnecessary Series Crossovers:** Surprisingly, *My Immortal* does a fairly good job of avoiding this problem. That is, until Morty Mcfli shows up with his blak tim machine to save the day. Yes, Marty Motherfucking McFly from *Back to the Future.* Apparently he's also now a goth and gave his Delorean a new black paint job to match the goffik nature of the story. There's also sort of a brief cameo by Tom Bombadil, of Lord of the Rings fame, except he is now just one of Voldemort's many alternate identities.

7. **Illogical Problem-Solving:** *"WE SEEM TO HAVE SOME EXTRA GOFFICK W8! WE NEED TO ALL GO ON GOFFIK ANOREXIA DIETS OR WE WILL SURELY LAND-CRASH!1"*

But it's really impossible to capture all of the insanity of *My Immortal* through words. You have to read it for yourself. So, without further ado, here is the worst fanfiction ever written.

Viower Excretion Advisd!

-Encyclopedia Dramatica

My Immortal

Chapter 1.

AN: Special fangz (get it, coz Im goffik) 2 my gf (ew not in that way) raven, bloodytearz666 4 helpin me wif da story and spelling. U rok! Justin ur da luv of my deprzzing life u rok 2! MCR ROX!

XX

Hi my name is Ebony Dark'ness Dementia Raven Way and I have long ebony black hair (that's how I got my name) with purple streaks and red tips that reaches my mid-back and icy blue eyes like limpid tears and a lot of people tell me I look like Amy Lee *(AN: if u don't know who she is get da hell out of here!)*. I'm not related to Gerard Way but I wish I was because he's a major fucking hottie. I'm a vampire but my teeth are straight and white. I have pale white skin. I'm also a witch, and I go to a magic school called Hogwarts in England where I'm in the seventh year (I'm seventeen). I'm a goth (in case you couldn't tell) and I wear mostly black. I love Hot Topic and I buy all my clothes from there. For example today I was wearing a black corset with matching lace around it and a black leather miniskirt, pink fishnets and black combat boots. I was wearing black lipstick, white foundation, black eyeliner and red eye shadow. I was walking outside Hogwarts. It was snowing and raining so there was no sun, which I was very happy about. A lot of preps stared at me. I put up my middle finger at them.

"Hey Ebony!" shouted a voice. I looked up. It was…. Draco Malfoy!

"What's up Draco?" I asked.

"Nothing." he said shyly.

But then, I heard my friends call me and I had to go away.

XXX

AN: IS it good? PLZ tell me fangz!

Chapter 2.

AN: Fangz 2 bloodytearz666 4 helpin me wif da chapta! BTW preps stop flaming ma story ok!

XXXXXXXXXXXXXXXXXXXXXXX666XXXXXXXXXXXXXXXXXXXXXXXXXX

The next day I woke up in my bedroom. It was snowing and raining again. I opened the door of my coffin and drank some blood from a bottle I had. My coffin was black ebony and inside it was hot pink velvet with black lace on the ends. I got out of my coffin and took of my giant MCR t-shirt which I used for pajamas. Instead, I put on a black leather dress, a pentagram necklace, combat boots and black fishnets on. I put on four pairs of earrings in my pierced ears, and put my hair in a kind of messy bun.

My friend, Willow *(AN: Raven dis is u!)* woke up then and grinned at me. She flipped her long waist-length raven black hair with pink streaks and opened her forest-green eyes. She put on her Marilyn Manson t-shirt with a black mini, fishnets and pointy high-heeled boots. We put on our makeup (black lipstick white foundation and black eyeliner.)

"OMFG, I saw you talking to Draco Malfoy yesterday!" she said excitedly.

"Yeah? So?" I said, blushing.

"Do you like Draco?" she asked as we went out of the Slytherin common room and into the Great Hall.

"No I so fucking don't!" I shouted.

"Yeah right!" she exclaimed. Just then, Draco walked up to me.

"Hi." he said.

"Hi." I replied flirtily.

"Guess what." he said.

"What?" I asked.

"Well, Good Charlotte are having a concert in Hogsmeade." he told me.

"Oh. My. Fucking. God!" I screamed. I love GC. They are my favorite band, besides MCR.

"Well…. do you want to go with me?" he asked.

I gasped.

Chapter 3.

AN: STOP FLAMMING DA STORY PREPZ OK! odderwize fangs 2 da goffik ppl 4 da good reveiws! FANGS AGEN RAVEN! oh yeah, BTW I don't own dis or da lyrics 4 Good Chralotte.

XXX

On the night of the concert I put on my black lace-up boots with high heels. Underneath them were ripped red fishnets. Then I put on a black leather minidress with all this corset stuff on the back and front. I put on matching fishnet on my arms. I straightened my hair and made it look all spiky. I felt a little depressed then, so I slit one of my wrists. I read a depressing book while I waited for it to stop bleeding and I listened to some GC. I painted my nails black and put on TONS of black eyeliner. Then I put on some black lipstick. I didn't put on foundation because I was pale anyway. I drank some human blood so I was ready to go to the concert.

I went outside. Draco was waiting there in front of his flying car. He was wearing a Simple Plan t-shirt (they would play at the show too), baggy black skater pants, black nail polish and a little eyeliner *(AN: A lot fo kewl boiz wer it ok!)*.

"Hi Draco!" I said in a depressed voice.

"Hi Ebony." he said back. We walked into his flying black Mercedes-Benz (the license plate said 666) and flew to the place with the concert. On the way we listened excitedly to Good Charlotte and Marilyn Manson. We both smoked cigarettes and drugs. When we got there, we both hopped out of the car. We went to the mosh pit at the front of the stage and jumped up and down as we listened to Good Charlotte.

"You come in cold, you're covered in blood
They're all so happy you've arrived
The doctor cuts your cord, hands you to your mom
She sets you free into this life." sang Joel *(I don't own da lyrics 2 dat song)*.

"Joel is so fucking hot." I said to Draco, pointing to him as he sung, filling the club with his amazing voice.

Suddenly Draco looked sad.

"What's wrong?" I asked as we moshed to the music. Then I caught on.

"Hey, it's ok I don't like him better than YOU!" I said.

"Really?" asked Draco sensitively and he put his arm around me all protective.

"Really." I said. "Besides I don't even know Joel and he's going out with Hilary fucking Duff. I fucking hate that little bitch." I said disgustedly, thinking of her ugly blonde face.

The night went on really well, and I had a great time. So did Draco. After the concert, we drank some beer and asked Benji and Joel for their autographs and photos with them. We got GC concert tees. Draco and I crawled back into the Mercedes-Benz, but Draco didn't go back into Hogwarts, instead he drove the car into.......................... the Forbidden Forest!

Chapter 4.

AN: I sed stup flaming ok ebony's name is ENOBY nut mary su OK! DRACO IS SOO IN LUV wif her dat he is acting defrent! dey nu eechodder b4 ok!

XXXXXXXXXXXXXXXXXX666XXXXXXXXXXXXXXXXXXXXX

"DRACO!" I shouted. "What the fuck do you think you are doing?"

Draco didn't answer but he stopped the flying car and he walked out of it. I walked out of it too, curiously.

"What the fucking hell?" I asked angrily.

"Ebony?" he asked.

"What?" I snapped.

Draco leaned in extra-close and I looked into his gothic red eyes (he was wearing color contacts) which revealed so much depressing sorrow and evilness and then suddenly I didn't feel mad anymore.

And then.............. suddenly just as I Draco kissed me passionately. Draco climbed on top of me and we started to make out keenly against a tree. He took of my top and I took of his clothes. I even took of my bra. Then he put his thingie into my you-know-what and we did it for the first time.

"Oh! Oh! Oh! " I screamed. I was beginning to get an orgasm. We started to kiss everywhere and my pale body became all warm. And then....

"WHAT THE HELL ARE YOU DOING YOU MOTHERFUKERS!"

It was..Dumbledore!

Chapter 5.

AN: STOP flaming! if u flam it menz ur a prep or a posr! Da only reson Dumbledeor swor is coz he had a hedache ok an on tup of dat he wuz mad at dem 4 having sexx! PS im nut updating umtil I get five good revoiws!

XXXXXXXXXXXXXXXXXXXXXX666XXXXXXXXXXXXXXXXXXXX

Dumbledore made and Draco and I follow him. He kept shouting at us angrily.

"You ludacris fools!" he shouted.

I started to cry tears of blood down my pallid face. Draco comforted me. When we went back to the castle Dumbledore took us to Professor Snape and Professor McGonagall who were both looking very angry.

"They were having sexual intercourse in the Forbidden Forest!" he yelled in a furious voice.

"Why did you do such a thing, you mediocre dunces?" asked Professor McGonagall.

"How dare you?" demanded Professor Snape.

And then Draco shrieked. "BECAUSE I LOVE HER!"

Everyone was quiet. Dumbledore and Professor McGonagall still looked mad but Professor Snape said. "Fine. Very well. You may go up to your rooms."

Draco and I went upstairs while the teachers glared at us.

"Are you okay, Ebony?" Draco asked me gently.

"Yeah I guess." I lied. I went to the girl's dorm and brushed my teeth and my hair and changed into a low-cut black floor-length dress with red lace all around it and black high heels. When I came out….

Draco was standing in front of the bathroom, and he started to sing 'I just wanna live' by Good Charlotte. I was so flattered, even though he wasn't supposed to be there. We hugged and kissed. After that, we said goodnight and he reluctantly went back into his room.

Chapter 6.

AN: shjt up prepz ok! PS I wnot update ubtil u give me goood revows!

XXXXXXXXXXXXXXXX666XXXXXXXXXXXXXXXXX

The next day I woke up in my coffin. I put on a black miniskirt that was all ripped around the end and a matching top with red skulls all over it and high heeled boots that were black. I put on two pairs of skull earrings, and two crosses in my ears. I spray-painted my hair with purple.

In the Great Hall, I ate some Count Chocula cereal with blood instead of milk, and a glass of red blood. Suddenly someone bumped into me. All the blood spilled over my top.

"Bastard!" I shouted angrily. I regretted saying it when I looked up cause I was looking into the pale white face of a gothic boy with spiky black hair with red streaks in it. He was wearing so much eyeliner that I was going down his face and he was wearing black lipstick. He didn't have glasses anymore and now he was wearing red contact lenses just like Draco's and there was no scar on his forhead anymore. He had a manly stubble on his chin. He had a sexy English accent. He looked exactly like Joel Madden. He was so sexy that my body went all hot when I saw him kind of like an erection only I'm a girl so I didn't get one you sicko.

"I'm so sorry." he said in a shy voice.

"That's all right. What's your name?" I questioned.

"My name's Harry Potter, although most people call me Vampire these days." he grumbled.

"Why?" I exclaimed.

"Because I love the taste of human blood." he giggled.

"Well, I am a vampire." I confessed.

"Really?" he whimpered.

"Yeah." I roared.

We sat down to talk for a while. Then Draco came up behind me and told me he had a surprise for me so I went away with him.

Chapter 7. Bring me 2 life

AN: wel ok u guyz im only writting dis cuz I got 5 god reviuws. n BTW I wont rite da nxt chapter til I git TIN god vons! STO FLAMING OR ILL REPORT U! Evony isn't a Marie Sue ok she isn't perfect SHES A SATANITS! n she has problemz shes depressed 4 godz sake!

XXXXXXXXXXXXXXXXXXXX666XXXXXXXXXZXXXXXXXXXXXXX

Draco and I held our pale white hands with black nail polish as we went upstairs. I was wearing red Satanist sings on my nails in red nail polish *(AN: c doez dat sound lik a Maru Sue 2 u?)*. I waved to Vampire. Dark misery was in his depressed eyes. I guess he was jealous of me that I was going out with Draco. Anyway, I went upstairs excitedly with Draco. We went into his room and locked the door. Then............

We started frenching passively and we took off each others clothes enthusiastically. He felt me up before I took of my top. Then I took off my black leather bra and he took off his pants. We went on the bed and started making out naked and then he put his boy's thingy in mine and we HAD SEX. *(c is dat stupid?)*

"Oh Draco, Draco!" I screamed while getting an orgasm when all of a sudden I saw a tattoo I had never seen before on Draco's arm. It was a black heart with an arrow through it. On it in bloody gothic writing were the words............ Vampire!

I was so angry.

"You bastard!" I shouted angrily, jumping out of the bed.

"No! No! But you don't understand!" Draco pleaded. But I knew too much.

"No, you fucking idiot!" I shouted. "You probably have AIDs anyway!"

I put on my clothes all huffily and then stomped out. Draco ran out even though he was naked. He had a really big you-know-what but I was too mad to care. I stomped out and did so until I was in Vampire's classroom where he was having a lesson with Professor Snape and some other people.

"VAMPIRE POTTER, YOU MOTHERFUCKER!" I yelled.

Chapter 8.

AN: stop flassing ok! if u do den u r a prep!

XXXXXXXXXXXXXXXXXXXXXXXXXXXX666XXXXXXXXXXX

Everyone in the class stared at me and then Draco came into the room even though he was naked and started begging me to take him back.

"Ebony, it's not what you think!" Draco screamed sadly.

My friend B'loody Mary Smith smiled at me understatedly. She flipped her long waste-length gothic black hair and opened her crimson eyes like blood that she was wearing contact lenses on. She had pale white skin that she was wearing white makeup on. Hermione was kidnapped when she was born. Her real parents are vampires and one of them is a witch but Voldemort killed her mother and her father committed suicide because he was depressed about it. She still has nightmares about it and she is very haunted and depressed. It also turns out her real last name is Smith and not Granger. (Since she has converted to Satanism she is in Slytherin now not Griffindoor.)

"What is it that you desire, you ridiculous dimwit!" Snape demeaned angrily in his cold voice but I ignored him.

"Vampire, I can't believe you cheated on me with Draco!" I shouted at him.

Everyone gasped.

I don't know why Ebony was so mad at me. I had went out with Vampire (I'm bi and so is Ebony) for a while but then he broke my heart. He dumped me because he liked Britney, a stupid preppy fucker. We were just good friends now. He had gone through horrible problems, and now he was gothic. (Haha, like I would hang out with a prep.)

"But I'm not going out with Draco anymore!" said Vampire.

"Yeah fucking right! Fuck off, you bastard!" I screamed. I ran out of the room and into the Forbidden Forest where I had lost my virility to Draco and then I started to bust into tears.

Chapter 9.

AN: stop flaming ok! I dntn red all da boox! dis is frum da movie ok so itz nut my folt if dumbeldor swers! besuizds I SED HE HAD A HEDACHE! and da reson snap dosent lik harry now is coz hes christian and vampire is a satanist! MCR ROX!

XXXXXXXXXXXXXXXXXX666XXXXXXXXXX

I was so mad and sad. I couldn't believe Draco for cheating on me. I began to cry against the tree where I did it with Draco.

Then all of a suddenly, an horrible man with red eyes and no nose and everything started flying towards me on a broomstick! He didn't have a nose *(basically like Voldemort in the movie)* and he was wearing all black but it was obvious he wasn't gothic. It was...... Voldemort!

"No!" I shouted in a scared voice but then Voldemort shouted "Imperius!" and I couldn't run away.

"Crookshanks!" I shouted at him. Voldemort fell of his broom and started to scream. I felt bad for him even though I'm a sadist so I stopped.

"Ebony." he yelled. "Thou must kill Vampire Potter!"

I thought about Vampire and his sexah eyes and his gothic black hair and how his face looks just like Joel Madden. I remembered that Draco had said I didn't understand, so I thought, what if Draco went out with Vampire before I went out with him and they broke up?

"No, Voldemort!" I shouted back.

Voldemort gave me a gun. "No! Please!" I begged.

"Thou must!" he yelled. "If thou does not, then I shall kill thy beloved

Draco!"

"How did you know?" I asked in a surprised way.

Voldemort got a dude-ur-so-retarded look on his face. "I hath telekinesis." he answered cruelly. "And if you doth not kill Vampire, then thou know what will happen to Draco!" he shouted. Then he flew away angrily on his broomstick.

I was so scared and mad I didn't know what to do. Suddenly Draco came into the woods.

"Draco!" I said. "Hi!"

"Hi." he said back but his face was all sad. He was wearing white foundation and messy eyeliner kind of like a pentagram *(geddit)* between Joel Madden and Gerard Way.

"Are you okay?" I asked.

"No." he answered.
"I'm sorry I got all mad at you but I thought you cheated on me." I expelled.

"That's okay." he said all depressed and we went back into Hogwarts together making out.

Chapter 10.

AN: stup it u gay fags if u donot lik ma story den fukk off! ps it turnz out b'loody mary isn't a muggle afert al n she n vampire r evil datz y dey movd houses ok!

XXXXXXXXXXXX666XXXXXXXXXXXXXX

I was really scared about Vlodemort all day. I was even upset went to rehearsals with my gothic metal band Bloody Gothic Rose 666. I am the lead singer of it and I play guitar. People say that we sound like a cross between GC, Slipknot and MCR. The other people in the band are B'loody Mary, Vampire, Draco, Ron (although we call him Diabolo now. He has black hair now with blue streaks in it.) and Hargrid. Only today Draco and Vampire were depressed so they weren't coming and we wrote songs instead. I knew Draco was probably slitting his wrists (he wouldn't die because he was a vampire too and the only way you can kill a vampire is with a c-r-o-s-s *(there's no way I'm writing that)* or a steak) and Vampire was probably watching a depressing movie like The Corpse Bride. I put on a black leather shirt that showed off my boobs and tiny matching miniskirt that said Simple Plan on the butt. You might think I'm a slut but I'm really not.

We were singing a cover of 'Helena' and at the end of the song I suddenly bust into tears.

"Ebony! Are you OK?" B'loody Mary asked in a concerted voice.

"What the fuck do you think?" I asked angrily. And then I said. "Well, Voldemort came and the fucking bastard told me to fucking kill Harry! But I don't want to kill him, because, he's really nice, even if he did go out with Draco. But if I don't kill Harry, then Voldemort, will fucking kill Draco!" I burst into tears.
Suddenly Draco jumped out from behind a wall.

"Why didn't you fucking tell me!" he shouted. "How could you- you- you fucking poser muggle bitch!" *(c is dat out of character?)*

I started to cry and cry. Draco started to cry too all sensitive. Then he ran out crying.

We practiced for one more hour. Then suddenly Dumbeldore walked in angrily! His eyes were all fiery and I knew this time it wasn't cause he had a headache.

"What have you done!" He started to cry wisely. *(c dats basically nut swering and dis time he wuz relly upset n u wil c y)* "Ebony Draco has been found in his room. He committed suicide by slitting his wrists."

Chapter 11.

AN: i sed stup flaming up prepz! c if dis chaptr is srupid!1111 it delz wit rly sris issus! sp c 4 urself if itz ztupid brw fangz 2 ma frend raven 4 hleping me!

XXXXXXXXXXXXXXXXX666XXXXXXXXXXXXXXXXXXXXXXX

"NO!" I screamed. I was horrorfied! B'loody Mary tried to comfort me but I told her fuck off and I ran to my room crying myself. Dumbledore chased after me shouting but he had to stop when I went into my room cause he would look like a perv that way.

Anyway, I started crying tears of blood and then I slit both of my wrists. They got all over my clothes so I took them off and jumped into the bath angrily while I put on a Linkin Park song at full volume. I grabbed a steak and almost stuck it into my heart to commit suicide. I was so fucking depressed! I got out of the bathtub and put on a black low-cut dress with lace all over it sandly. I put on black high heels with pink metal stuff on the ends and six pairs of skull earrings. I couldn't fucking believe it. Then I looked out the window and screamed... Snap was spying on me and he was taking a video tape of me! And Loopin was masticating to it! They were sitting on their broomsticks.

"EW, YOU FUCKING PERVS, STOP LOOKING AT ME NAKED! ARE YOU PEDOS OR WHAT!" I screamed putting on a black towel with a picture of Marilyn Mason on it. Suddenly Vampire ran in.

"Abra Kedavra!" he yelled at Snape and Loopin pointing his womb. I took my gun and shot Snape and Loopin a gazillion times and they both started screaming and the camera broke. Suddenly, Dumblydore ran in. "Ebony, it has been revealed that someone has - NOOOOOOOOOOOOOO!" he shouted looking at Snape and Loopin and then he waved his wand and suddenly...

Hargrid ran outside on his broom and said everyone we need to talk.

"What do you know, Hargrid? You're just a little Hogwarts student!"

"I MAY BE A HOGWARTS STUDENT...." Hargirid paused angrily. "BUT I AM ALSO A SATANIST!"

"This cannot be." Snap said in a crisp voice as blood dripped from his hand where Dumblydore's wand had shot him. "There must be other factors."

"YOU DON'T HAVE ANY!" I yelled in madly.

Loopin held up the camera triumelephantly. "The lens may be ruined but the tape is still there!"

I felt faint, more than I normally do like how it feels when you do not drink enough blood.

"Why are you doing this?" Loopin said angrily while he rubbed his dirty hands on his clook.

And then I heard the words that I had heard before but not from him. I did not know whether to feel shocked and happy or to bite him and drink his blood because I felt faint.

"BECAUSE...BECAUSE...." Hargid said and he paused in the air dramitaclly, waving his wand in the air. Then swooped he in singing to the tune of a gothic version of a song by 50 Cent.

"Because you're goffic?" Snap asked in a little afraid voice cause he was afraind it meant he was connected with Satan.

"Because I LOVE HER!"

Chapter 12.

AN: stop f,aing ok hargrid is a pedo 2 a lot of ppl in amerikan skoolz r lik dat I wunted 2 adres da ishu! how du u no snap iant kristian plus hargrid isn't really in luv wif ebony dat was sedric ok!

XXXXXXXXXXXX666XXXXXXXXXXXXXXXXX

I was about to slit my wrists again with the silver knife that Drago had given me in case anything happened to him. He had told me to use it valiantly against an enemy but I knew that we must both go together.

"NO!" I THOUGHT IT WAS HAIRgrid but it was Vampire. He started to scream. "OMFG! NOOOOO! MY SCAR HURTS!" and then..... his eyes rolled up! You could only see his red whites.

I stopped. "How did u know?"

"I saw it! And my scar turned back into the lightning bolt!"

"NO!" I ran up closer. "I thought you didn't have a scar anymore!" I shouted.

"I do but Diabolo changed it into a pentagram for me and I always cover it up with foundation." he said back. "Anyway my scar hurt and it turned back into the lightning bolt! Save me! then I had a vision of what was happening to Draco...............Volfemort has him bondage!"

Anyway I was in the school nurse's office now recovering from my slit wrists. Snap and Loopin and HAHRID were there too. They were going to St. Mango's after they recovered cause they were pedofiles and you can't have those fucking pervs teaching in a school with lots of hot gurlz. Dumbledore had constipated the cideo camera they took of me naked. I put up my middle finger at them.

Anyway Hargrid came into my hospital bed holding a bouquet of pink roses.

"Enoby I need to tell u somethnig." he said in a v. serious voice, giving me the roses.

"Fuck off." I told him. "You know I fucking hate the color pink anyway, and I don't like fucked up preps like you." I snapped. Hargrid had been mean to me before for being gottik.

"No Enoby." Hargrid says. "Those are not roses."

"What, are they goffs too you poser prep?" I asked cause I was angry that he had brought me pink roses.

"I saved your life!" He yelled angrily. "No you didn't I replied." "You saved me from getting a Paris Hilton p- video made from your shower scene and being vued by Snap and Loopin." Who MASTABATED *(c is dat speld rong)* to it he added silently.

"Whatever!" I yelled angirly.
He pointed his wand at the pink roses. "These aren't roses." He suddenly looked at them with an evil look in his eye and muttered Well If you wanted Honesty that's all you haD TO SAY! .

"That's not a spell that's an MCR song." I corrected him wisely.

"I know, I was just warming up my vocal cordes." Then he screamed. "Petulus merengo mi kremicli romacio*(4 all u cool goffic mcr fans out, there, that is a tribute! specially for raven I love you girl!)*imo noto okayo!"

And then the roses turned into a huge black flame floating in the middle of the air. And it was black. Now I knew he wasn't a prep.

"OK I believe you now wtf is Drako?"

Hairgrid rolled his eyes. I looked into the balls of flame but I could c nothing.

"U c, Enobby," Dumblydore said, watching the two of us watching the flame. "2 c wht iz n da flmes*(HAHA U REVIEWRS FLAMES GEDDIT)* u mst find urslf 1st, k?"

"I HAVE FOUND MYSELF OK YOU MEAN OLD MAN!" Hargrid yelled. dUMBLydore lookd shockd. I guess he didn't have a headache or else he would have said something back.

Hairgrid stormed off back into his bed. "U r a liar, prof dumbledoree!"

Anyway when I got better I went upstairs and put on a black leather minidress that was all ripped on the ends with lace on it. There was some corset stuff on the front. Then I put on black fishnets and black high-heeled boots with pictures of Billie Joe Armstrong on them. I put my hair all out around me so I looked like Samara from the Ring *(if u don't know who she iz ur a prep so fuk off!)* and I put on blood-red lipstick, black eyeliner and black lip gloss.

"You look kawai, girl." B'loody Mary said sadly. "Fangs *(geddit)* you do too." I said sadly too, but I was still upset. I slit both of my wrists feeling totally depressed and I sucked all the blood. I cried again in my bathroom and put the shades on so Snap and Loopin couldn't spy on me this time. I went to some classes. Vampire was in the Hair of Magical Magic Creatures. He looked all depressed because Draco had disappeared and he had used to be in love with Draco. He was sucking some blood from a Hufflepuff.

"Hi." he said in a depressed way. "Hi back." I said in an wqually said way.

We both looked at each other for some time. Harry had beautiful red gothic eyes so much like Dracos. Then......... we jumped on each other

xxx

and started screwing each other.

"STOP IT NOW YOU HORNY SIMPLETONS!" shouted Professor McGoggle who was watching us and so was everyone else.

"Vampire you fucker!" I said slapping him. "Stop trying to screw me. You know I loved Draco!" I shouted and then I ran away angrily.

Just then he started to scream. "OMFG! NOOOOO! MY SCAR HURTS!" and then..... his eyes rolled up! You could only see his red whites.

"NO!" I ran up closer.

"I thought you didn't have a scar anymore!" I shouted.

"I do but Diabolo changed it into a pentagram for me and I always cover it up with foundation." he said back. "Anyway my scar hurt and then I had a vision of what was happening to Draco...............Volfemort has him bondage!"

XXXXXXXXXXXXXXXXXX666XXXXXXXXXX

SPECIAL FANGZ 2 RAVEN MY GOFFIX BLOOD SISTA WTF UR SUPPOZD 2 RIT DIS!11111111

HEY RAVEN DO U KNOW WHERE MY SWEATER I

Chapter 13.

AN: raven fangz 4 gelpin me agen im sory ah tok ur postr of gerard but dat guy is such a fokin sexbom! PREPZ STOP FLAMIGNG!

XXXXXXXXXXXXXXXXX666XXXXXXXXXXXXXXXXXX

Vampire and I ran up the stairs looking for Dumbledore. We were so scared.

"Dumbledore Dumblydore!" we both yelled. Dumbledore came there.

"What is it that you want now you despicable snobs?" he asked angrily.

"Volsemort has Draco!" we shouted at the same time.

He laughed in an evil voice.

"No! Don't! We need to save Draco!" we begged.

"No." he said meanly. "I don't give a darn what Voldemort does to Draco. Not after how much he misbehaved in school especially with YOU Ebony." he said while he frowned looking at me. "Besides I never liked him that much anyway." then he walked away. Vampire started crying. "My Draco!" he moaned. *(AN: don't u fik gay guyz r lik so hot!)*

"Its okay!" I tried to tell him but that didn't stop him. He started to cry tears of blood. Then he had a brainstorm. "I had an idea!" he exclaimed.

"What?" I asked him.

"You'll see." he said. He took out his wand and did a spell. Then...... suddenly we were in Voldemprt's lair!

We ran in with our wands out just as we heard a croon voice say. "Allah Kedavra!"

It was…………………………….. Voldemort!

Chapter 14.

AN: *fuk off PREPZ ok! Raven fangz 4 helpin agen. im sory ah kudnt update but I wuz derperessd n I had 2 go 2 da hospital kuz I slit muh rists. PS im nut updating til u giv me 10 god revoiws!*

XXXXXXXXXXXXXXXXXXX666XXXXXXXXXX

WARNING: SUM OF DIS CHAPTA IS XTREMLY SCRAY. VIOWER EXCRETION ADVISD.

We ran to where Volcemort was. It turned out that Voldemort wasn't there. Instead the fat guy who killed Cedric was. Draco was there crying tears of blood. Snaketail was torturing him. Vampire and I ran in front of Snaketail.

"Rid my sight you despicable preps!" he shouted as we started shooting him with the gun he Then suddenly he looked at me and he fell down with a lovey-dovey look in his eyes.
"Ebonylloveyouwiluhavesexwithme." he said. *(in dis he is sixteen yrs old so hes not a pedofile ok)*

"Huh?" I asked.
"Enoby I love you will you have sex with me?" asked Snaketail. I started laughing crudely. "What the fuck? You torture my bf and then you expect me to fuck you? God, you are so fucked up you fucking bastard." I said angrily. Then I stabbed him in the heart. Blood pored out of it like a fountain.

"Nooooooooooooo!" he screamed. He started screaming and running around. Then he fell down and died. I brust into tears sadly.

"Snaketail what art thou doing?" called Voldemort. Then...... he started coming! We could hear his high heels clacking to us. So we got on our broomsticks and we flew to Hogwarts. We went to my room. Vampire went away. There I started crying.

"What's wrong honey?" asked Draco taking off his clothes so we could screw. He had a sex-pack *(geddit cuz hes so sexah)* and a really huge you-know-what and everything.

"Its so unfair!" I yielded. "Why can't I just be ugly or plain like all da other girls and preps here except for B'loody Mary, because she's not ugly or anything."

"Why would you wanna be ugly? I don't like the preps anyway. They are such fucking sluts." answered Draco.

"Yeah but everyone is in love with me! Like Snape and Loopin took a video of me naked. Hargrid says he's in love with me. Vampire likes me and now even Snaketail is in love with me! I just wanna be with you ok Draco! Why couldn't Satan have made me less beautiful?" I shouted angrily. *(an" don't wory enoby isn't a snob or anyfing but a lot of ppl hav told her shes pretty)* "Im good at too many things! WHY CAN'T I JUST BE NORMAL? IT'S A FUCKING CURSE!" I shouted and then I ran away.

Chapter 15.

AN: stup flaming ok! btw u suk frum no on evry tim sum1 flams me im gona slit muh ristsz! fangz 2 raven 4 hlpein!

XXXXXXXXXXXXX666XXXXXXXXXXXXXX

"Ebony Ebony!" shouted Draco sadly. "No, please, come back!"

But I was too mad.

"Whatever! Now u can go anh have sex with Vampire!" I shouted. I stormed into my room and closed my black door with my blood-red key. It had a picture of Marylin Manson on it. He looked so sexy in a way that reminded me of Draco and Vampire. I started to cry and weep. I took a razor and started to slit my wrists. I drank the blood all depressed. Then I looked at my black GC watch and noticed it was time to go to Biology class.

I put on a short ripped black gothic dress that said Anarchy on the front in blood red letters and was all ripped and a spiky belt. Under that I put on ripped black fishnets and boots that said Joel all over them with blood red letters. I put my ebony black hair out. Anyway I went downstairs feeling all sad and depressed as usual. I did sum advanced Biology work. I was turning a bloody pentagram into a black guitar. Suddenly the guitar turned to Draco!

"Enoby I love you!" he shouted sadly. "I dnot care what those fucker preps and posers fink. Ur da most beautiful girl in the world. Before I met you I used to want to commit suicide all the time. Now I just wanna fucking be with you. I fucking love you!." Then............... he started to sing "Da Chronicles of Life and Death" (we considered it our song now cuz we fell in love when Joel was singing it) right in front of the entire class! His singing voice was so amazing and gothic and sexxy like a cross between Gerard, Joel, Chester, Pierre and Marilyn Manson *(AN: don't u fink dos guyz r so hot. if u dnot no who dey r get da fuk out od hr!)* .

"OMFG." I said after he was finished. Some fucking preps stared at us but I just stuck up my middle fingers (that were covered in black nail polish and were entwined with Draco's now) at them. "I love you!" I said and then we started to kiss just like Hilary Duff (i fukin h8 dat bitch) and CMM in a Cinderella Story. Then we went away holding hands. Loopin shouted at us but he stopped cuz everyone was clapping by how sexy we looked 2gether. Then I saw a poster saying that MCR would have a concert in Hogsmede right then. We looked at each other all shocked and then we went 2gether.

Chapter 16.

AN: u no wut! sut up ok! proov 2 me ur nut prepz! raven u suk u fuken bich gimme bak mah fukijn swteet ur supsd 2 rit dis! Raven wtf u bich ur suposd to dodis! BTW fangz 2 britney5655 4 techin muh japnese!

XXXXXXXXXXXXX666XXXXXXXXXXXXXX

We ran happily to Hogsmede. There we saw the stage where GC had played. We ran in happly. MCR were there playing 'Helena'. I was so fucking happy! Gerard looked even sexier than he did in da pictures. Even Draco thought so, I could totally see him getting an erection but it didn't matter cuz I knew know that we were da only true ones for eachother. I was wearing a black leather minidress and black leather platinum boots with red ripped fishnets. Draco was wearing a black baggy MCR t-shirt and black baggy pants. Anyway, we stated moshing to Helena. We frenched. We ran up 2 the front of the band to stage-dive. Suddenly, Gerard pulled off his mask. So did the others. We gasped. It wasn't them at all. It was.,........................... Volsemort and da Death Dealers!

"Wtf Draco im not going to a concert wid u!" I shouted angrily. "Not after what happened to me last time? Even if its MCR n u no how much I lik them"

"What cause we...you know..." he gadgetted uncomfortbli cause guys don't like to talk a bout you-know-what.

"Yeah cause we you know!" I yielded in an angry voice.

"We won't do that again." Draco promised. "This time, we're going with an ESCORT."

"OMFG wtf/ Are you giving into the mainstream?" I asked. "So I guess ur a prep or a Christina or what now?"

"NO." he muttered loudly.

"R u becoming a prep or what?" I shootd angrily.

"Enoby! I'm not! Pls come with me!" He fell down to his knees and started singing 'Da world is black' by GC to me.

I was flattened cause that's not even a single, he had memorized da lyrks just 4 me!

"OK then I guess I will have to." I said and then we frenched 4 a while and I went up 2 my room.

B'loody Mary was standing there. "Hajimemashite gurl." she said happily (she spex Japanese so do i. dat menz 'how do u do' in japanese). "BTW Willow that fucking poser got expuld. she failed al her klasses and she skepped math." *(an: RAVEN U FUKIN SUK! FUK U!)*

"It serves that fuking bich right." I laughed angrily.

Well anyway we where felling all deprezzed. We wutsched some goffic movies like Das niteMARE b4 xmas. "Maybe Willow will die too." I said.

"Kawai." B'loody Mair shook her head enrgtically lethrigcly. "Oh yeah o have a confession after she got expuld I murdered her and den loopin did it with her cause he's a necphilak."

"Kawai." I commnted happily . We talked to each other in silence for da rest uv da movie.

"OH HEY BTw, im going to a concert with drako tonight in Hogsmeade with mcr." I sed. " I need to wear like da hotset outfit EVA."

B'Loody Mairy Nodded ENREGeticALLIY. "Omfg totally lets go shopping."

"In Hot Topic, right?" I asked, already getting out my spshcial Hot Topic Loiyalty carde.

"No." My head snaped up.

'WHAT?" my head spuin. I could not believe it. "B'Loody Mary are u a PREP?"

"NOOOO!NOOOO!" She laughed. "I found some cool goffic stores near Hogwarts that's all."

"Hu told u abut them" I askd sure it would be Drako or Diabolo or Vampire(don't even SAY that nam to me!). Or me.

"Dumblydore." She sed. "Let me just call our broms."

"OMFFG DUMBLYDORE?" I asked quietly.

"Yah I saw the map for Hogsmeade on his desk." She told me. "Come on let's go."

We were going in a few punkgoff stores SPECIALLY for the concerts in Hogsmeade. The salesperson was OMG HOTTER THAN GERARD EXCEPT NOT CAUSE THAT'S IMPOSSIBLE and he gave me a few dresses. "We only have these for da real goffs."

"Da real goffs?" Me and B'Loody Mary asked.

"Yah u wouldn't believe how many posers ther are in this town man! Yesterday loopin and snap tried to buy a goffic camera pouch." He shook his head. "I dint even no they had a camera."

"OMFG NO THEIR GONNA SPY ON ME AGAIN!" I cried, running out of the changing room wearing a long black dress with lots of red tulle

coming out and very low-cut with a huge slit.

"Oh my satan you have to buy that outfit" The salesperson said.

"Yeah it looks totlly hot." said B'Loody Mary.

"You know what I am gona give it to you free cause u look really hot in that utfit. Hey are you gonna be at the concert tonight?" he asked. "Yeah I am actually." I looked back at him. "Hey BTW my name's ebondy dark'ness dementia TARA way what's yours?"

"Tom Rid." He said and ran a hand through his black-dyed hair. "maybe I'll see you there tonight."

"Yeah I don't think so cause I am going there with my bf drako you sick perv!" I yelled angrily, but before he could beg me to go with him, Hargrid flew in on his black broom looking worried. "OMFG EBONDY U NEED OT GET BACK INTO THE CASTLE NOW!"

Chapter 17.

AN: I sed stup flming da stryo! if ur a prep den dnot red it! u kin tel weder ur a prep or not by ma quiz itz on ma hompage. if ur not den u rok. if u r den FOOOOOK UFFFFFFFFFF! pz willo isn't rely a prep. Raven plz do dis il promis 2 giv u bak ur postr!

XXXXXXXXXXXXXXXXXXXXXXX666XXXXXXXXXXXXXXX

Tom Riddle gave us some clothes n stuff 4 free. He said he wud help us wif makeup if he wunted koz he was relly in2 fashin n stuff. (hes bisezual). Hargird kept shooting at us to cum back 2 Hogwarts. "WTF Hargrid?" I shouted angrily. "Fuck off you fjucking bastard." Well anyway Willow came. Hargird went away angrily.

"Hey bitch you look kawaii." she said.

"Yah but not as kawaii as you." I answered sadly cause Willow's really pretty and everything. She was wearing a short black corset-thingy with blood red lace on it and a blak blood-red miniskirt, leather fish-nets and black poiny boots that showed off how pale she wuz. She had a really nice body wif big bobs and everything. She was thin enouff 2 be anorexic.

"So r u going 2 da concert wif Draco?" she asked.

"Yah." I said happily.

"I'm gong with Diabolo." she anserred happily. Well anyway Draco and Diabolo came. They were both loking extremely hot and sexy and u could tell they thoufht we were ot 2. Diabolo was wearing a black t-shirt that said '666' on it. He was wearing tons off makeup jus like Marylin Manson. Draco was wearing black leather pants, a gothic black GC t-shirt and black Vans he got from da Warped tower. B'loody Mart was going 2 da concert wif Dracola. Dracola used to be called Navel but it tuned out dat he was kidnapped at birth and his real family were vampires. They dyed in a car crash. Navel converted to Satanism and he

went goth. He was in Slitherin now. He was wearing a black Wurped t-shirt, black jeans and shoes and black hair wif red streekz in it. We kall him Dracula now. Well anyway we al went 2 Draco's black Mercy-Bens (geddit cuz wer gpffik) that his dad Lucian gave him. We did pot, coke and crak. Draco and I made out. We made fun of dose stupid fuking preps. We soon got there.......I gapsed.

Gerard was da sexiest guy eva! He locked even sexier den he did in pix. He had long raven blak hair n piercing blue eyes. He wuz really skinny and he had n amazing ethnic voice. We moshed 2 Helena and sum odder songz. Sudenly Gerard polled of his mask. So did the other membez. I gasped. It wasn't Gerard at all! It was an ugly preppy man wif no nose and red eyes... Every1 ran away but me and Draco. Draco and I came. It was.......Vlodemort and da Death Deelers!

"U moronic idiots!" he shooted angstily. "Enoby, I told u to kill Vampire. Thou have failed. And now..........I shall kill thou and Draco!"

"No no please!" We begged sadly but he took out his knife.

Sudenly a gothic old man flu in on his broomstick. He had lung black hair and a looong black bread. He wus werring a blak robe dat sed 'avril lavigne' on da back. He shotted a spel and Vlodemort ran away. It was.................................DUMBLYDORE!

Chapter 18.

AN: I SED STUP FLAMMING! if u do den ur a fuken prep! fangz 2 raven 4 da help n stuf. u rok! n ur nut a prep. fangz for muh sewter! ps da oder eson dumbeldor swor is koz he trin 2 be gofik so der!

XXXXXXXXXXXX666XXXXXXXXXXXXXXXXX

I woke up the next day in my coffin. I walked out of it and put on some black eyeliner, black eyesharrow, blood-bed lipstick and a black really low-cut leather dress that was all ripped and in stripes so you could see my belly. I was wearing a skull belly ring with black and red diamonds inside it.

(Da night before Draco and I rent back to the skull *(geddit skull koz im goffik n I like deth)*. Dumbeldore chased Vlodemort away. We flew there on our brooms. Mine was black and the broom-stuff was blood-red. There was lace all over it. Draco had a black MCR boom. We went back to our rooms and we had you-know-what to a Linkin Park song.)

Well anyway I went down to the Grate Hall. There all da walls were painted black and da tables were black too. But you fould see that there was pink pant underneath the black pant. And there were pastors of poser bands everywhere, like Ashlee Simpson and the Backstreet Boys.

"WTF!" I shouted going to sit next to B'loody Mary and Willow. B'loody Mary was wearing a black leather mini with a Good Chraloote t-shirt, black fishnets and black pointy boots. Willow was wearing a long gothic blak dress with blood red writing that was all lacy and came up to your thighs and black boots and fishnets. Vampire, Dracula and Draco came. We started to talk about who was sexier, Mikey or Gerard Way or Billie Joe Armstrong. The boys joined in cause they were bi.

"Those guys are so fucking hot." Navel was saying as suddenly a gothic old man with a black beard and everything came. He was the same one who had chassed away Vlodemort yesterday. He had normal tan skin

but he was wearing white foundation and he had died his hare black.

"...................DUMBLEDORE?1!" we all gasped.

"WTF?" I shouted angrily. "I thought he was just wearing that to scare Volsemort!"

"Hello everyone." he said happily. "As u can see I gave the room a makeover. Whjat do u fink about it?"

Everyone from the poser table in Gryiffindoor started to cheer. Well we goths just looked at each other all disfusted and shook our heads. We couldn't believe what a poser he was!1.

"BTW you can call me Albert." HE CALLED AS WE LEFT to our classes.

"What a fucking poser!" Draco shouted angrily as we we to Transfomation. We were holding hands. Vampire looked really jealous. I could see him crying blood in a gothic way *(geddit, way lik Gerard)* but I didn't say anything. "I bet he's havin a mid-life crisis!" Willow shouted.

I was so fucking angry.
Chapter 19. im nut ok i promise

AN: plz stup flaming da story if u do ur a foken prep n ur jelous ok!11 frum noq un im gong 2 delt ur men reviowz!111 BTW evonyd a poorblod so der!1 fangz 2 raven 4m da help!11

XXXXXXXXXXXXXXXX666XXXXXXXXXXXXXXXXXX

All day we sat angerly finking about Dumbelldore. We were so fucking pissed off. Well, I had one thing to look forward too- da MCR concert. It had been postphoned, so we could all go.

Anyway, I went to the common room sadly to cut classes. Draco was

being all secretive.

I asked what it was and he got all mad me and started crying all hot and angsty (rnt sensitve bi guyz so hot).

"No one fucking understands me!1" he shouted angrily as his black hare went in his big blue eyes like Billie Joe in Boulevard of Borken Dreamz. He was wearing black baggy paints, a black MCR t-shirt and a black die. *(geddit insted of tie koz im goffik)* I was wearing a blak leather low cut top with chains all over it all over it a blak leather mini, black high held boots and a cross belly fing. My hair was al up in a messy relly high bun like Amy Lee in Gong Under. *(email me if u wana see da pik)*

"Accuse me? What about me!" I growled.

"Buy-but-but-" he grunted.

"You fucking bastard!" I moaned.

"No! Wait! It's not what it fucking looks like!" he shouted.

But it was to late. I knew what I herd. I ran to the bathroom angrily, cring. Draco banged on the door. I whipped and whepped as my blody eyeliner streammed down my cheeks and made cool tears down my feces like Benji in the video for Girls and Bois *(raven that is soo our video!).* I TOOOK OUT A CIGARETE END STARTED TO smoke pot.

Suddenly Hargrid came. He had appearated.

"You gave me a fucking shock!" I shouted angrily dropping my pot. "Wtf do you fink you're doing in da gurl's room?"

Only it wasn't just Hargrid. Someone else was with him too! For a second I wanted it 2 b Tom Rid or maybe Draco but it was Dumblydore.

"Hey I need to ask you a question." he said, pulling out his black wanabe-goffik purse. "What are u wearing to the concert?"

"U no who MCR r!" I gasped.

"No I just saw there was a concert dat a lot of gothz and punx were going 2." He said. "Anyway Draco has a surprise for u."

Chapter 20.

AN: I sed I dnoty ker wut u fink! stof pflamin ok prepz!1 fangz 2 raven 4 da help!1 oh yah btw ill be un vacation in transilvania 4 da nex 3 dayz so dnot expect updatz.

XXXXXXXXXXXXXXXXXXXXX666XXXXXXXXXXXXXX

All day I wondered what the surprise was. Meanwhile, I pot on a blak ledder mini, a blak corset with urple lace stuff all over it, an black gothic compact boots. MCR were gong 2 do the concert again, since Volxemort had taken over the last one. I slit my wrists while I moshed 2 MCR in my bedroom all night, feeling excited. Suddenly someone knocked on the door while I was trying on sum black clothes and moshing to Fang u 4 da Venom. I gut all mad and turned it of, but sacredly I hopped inside dat it was Draco so we could do it again.

"Wut de fucking hell r u doing!" I shouted angrily. It was Loopin! "R u gonna cum rape me or what." I yelled. I was allowed to say dat because Dumblydore had told us all 2 be careful around hem and Snap since he was a pedo.

"No, actshelly *(geddit, hell)* kan I plz burrow sum condemns." he growld angrily.

"Yah, so u can fuk ur six-yr-old gurlfriend, huh?" I shouted sarkastikally.

"Fuker." He said, gong away.

Well anyway, I put on some black eyesharow, black eyeliner, and some black lipstick and white foundation. Then I went. Den I gasped...Snake and Loopin were in da middle of da empty hall, doin it, and Dobby was watching!1

"Oh my god you ludacris idiot!" they both shooted angrily when they saw me. Dobby ran away crying. Dey got up, though. Normally I wood have ben turned on (I luv cing guyz do it) but both of them were fuking

preps. (btw snake is movd 2 griffindoor now)

"WTF is that why u wanted condoms?" I asked sadistically. *(c I speld dat)*

"Only you wouldn't give them to me!" Lumpkin shouted angrily.

"Well you shoulda told me." I replayed.

"You dimwit!." Snake began 2 shoot angrily. And then.........I took out my black camera and took a pic of them. U could see that they were naked and everything.

"Well xcuse me!" they both shouted angrily. "What was dat al about?"

"It wuz to blackmail u." I snarked. "So now next time you see me doing it with my boyfriend you cant fuking rat me out or I'll show dis to Dumbledork. So fuck off, u bastards!" I started to run. They chased me but I threw my wound at them and dey tripped over it. Well anyway, I went outside and there was Vampire, looking extremely fucking hot. "WTF where'd Draco?" I asked him.

"Oh he's bein a fucking bastard. He told me he wouldn't cum." Vampire said shaking his hed. "U wanna cum with me? 2 the concert?"

Then..... he showed me his flying car. I gasped. It was a black car. He said his dogfather Serious Blak had given it 2 him. The license plate on the front sed MCR666 on it. The one on da back said 'ENOBY' on it.

..........I gasped.

We flew to the concert hall. MCR were there, playing.

Vampire and I began 2 make out, moshing to the muzik. I gapsed, looking at da band.

I almost had an orgasim. Gerard was so fucking hot! He begin 2 sing 'Helena' and his sexah beautiful voice began 2 fill the hall.And den, I heard some crrying. I turned and saw Draco, cryin in a corner.

Chapter 21.

AN: *fuk u ok! u fokng suk. itz nut ma fult if itz speld rong ok koz dat bich ravern*

cuz it fok u prepz!1 woopz soz raven fangz 4 da help. btw transilvana rox hrad!1
I even gut 2 go 2 da kasel wer drkola was flimed!

XXXXXXXXXXXXXXXXXXXXX666XXXXXXXXXXXXXXX

Later we all went in the skull. Draco was crying in da common room. "Draco are u okay?" I asked in a gothic voice.

"No I'm not u fuking bitch!" he shouted angrily. He stated to run out of the place in a suicidal way. I stated to cry cuz I was afraid he would commit suicide.

"Its ok Enoby." said Vampire comfortly. "Ill make him feel better."

"U mean you'll go fuck him wont you!" I shouted angrily. Then I ran 2 get Draco. Vampire came too.

"Draco please come!" he began to cry. Tears of blood came down his pail face. I wuz so turned on cuz I love sensitive bi guyz. (if ur a homophone den fuk of!)

And then............................. we herd sum footsteps! Vampire got out his blak invincibility coke. We both gut under it. We saw the janitor Mr. Norris there, shouting angrily with a flashlight in his hand.

"WHOSE THERE!" he shouted angrily. We saw Filth come. He went unda da invisibility cloke and started to meow loudly.

"IS ANY1 THERE!" yelled Mr. Norris.

"No fuck u you preppy little poser sun of a fukcing bich!" Vampire said under his breast in a disgusted way.

"EXCUS ME! EXCUS ME WHO SED DAT!" yelled Mr. Norris. Den he heard Filch meow. "Filth is der any1 unda da cloak!" he asked. Filth nodded.

And then………………………Vampir frenched me! He did it jus
as……………………. Mr. Norris was taking of da cloak!1

"WHAT DA-" he yelled but it was 2 late cuz now we were ruining away
frum him. And den we saw Draco crying n bustin in2 tearz and slitting
his rists outside of da school.

"Draco!" I cried. "R u okay?"

"I guess though." Draco weeped. We went back to our coffins frenching
each other. Draco and I decided to watch Lake Placid *(c isnt da deprezzin)*
on the gothic red bed together. As I wuz about 2 put in the video, my
eyes rolled up and suddenly I had a vision of something that was
happening now. There was a knok on the door and Fug and da Mystery
of Magic walked into the school!1

Chapter 22.

AN: stfu! prepz stup flaming ok if u dnot lik it fuk of I no itz mr. noris itz raven's folt ok!11 u suk!1 no jus kidding raven u fokieng rok prepz suk!1

XXXXXXXXXXXXXXXXX666XXXXXXXXXXXXXXXXXXXXXXXXXXXX

All day everyone talked about the Misery of Magic. Well anyway, I woke up the next day. I was in my coffin so I opened the door. I was wearing blak lacey leather pajamas. Then I gasped.

Standing in front of me where................... B;loody Mary, Vampire, Diabolo, Draco, Dracula and Willow!

I opened my crimson eyes. Willow was wearing a tight black leather top with pictures of bloody roses all over it. Under that she wart a black poofy skirt wit lace on it and black gothic boots that was attached to the top. Vampire was wearing a baggy Simple Plan t-shirt and baggy black pants and Vans. Draco was wearing a black MCR t-shirt and blak jeans and a leather jacket. He looked just likee Gerard Way, and almost as fucking sexy. Vampire looked like Joel Madden. B'loody Mary was wearing a tight black poofy gothic dress that she had ripped so it showed of all her clearage with a white apron that said 'bich' and other swear words and MCR lyrics on it kind of like one dress I had seen Amy Lee wear once. Darkness (who is Jenny) was there too. She was weaving a ripped gothic black dress with ripped stuff all over it and a lace-up top thing and black pointy boots. So were Crab and Goyle. It turns out that Darkness, Diabolo, Crab and Goyle's dad was a vampire. He committed suicide by slitting his wrists with a razor. He had raped them and stuff before too. They all got so depressed that they became goffik and converted to Stanism.

"OMFG" I yielded as I jumped up. "Why the fuck are u all here?"

"Enoby something is really fucked up." Draco said.

"OK but I need to put my fucking clothes on first." I shouted angrily.

"It's all right. We have to go now and you look kawaii anyway. Your so fucking beautiful." Draco said in a sexy voice.

"Oh all right." I said smiling. "But you have to tell me why your being all erective."

"I will I will." he said.

So I just put on some black eyeliner, black lipstick and red eyeshadow and white foundation. Then I came. We all went outside the Great Hal and looked in from a widow. A fucking prep called Britney from Griffindoor was standing next to us. She was wearing a pink mini and a Hilary Duff t-shirt so we put up our middle fingers at her. Inside the Great Hall we could see Dumbledork. Cornelia Fudged was there shouting at Dumbledore. Doris Rumbridge was there too.

"THIS CANNOT BE!" she shouted angrily. "THE SCHOOL MUST BE CLOSED!"

"THE BARK LORD IS PLANNING TO KILL THE STUDENTS!" yelled Cornelia Fudge.

"YOU ARE NOT FIT TO BE THE PRINCIPAL ANY LONGER!" yelled Rumbridge. "YOU ARE TOO OLD AND YOUR ALZHEIMERS IS DANGEROUS! YOU MUST RETRY OR VOLDEMORT WILL KILL YOUR STUDENTS!"

"Very well." Dumbledore said angrily. "Butt we cannot do this. We can't close the school. There is only one person who is capable of killing Voldemort and she is in the school. And her name is...Enony Dark'ness Dementia Raven Way."

Draco, Crab, Goyle, Darkness, Willow, Vampire and B'loody Mary looked

at each other………I gasped.

Chapter 23.

AN: dhut da fok up biches!1 ur jus jelos koz I gut 10000 reviowz!1 fangz 2 raven 4 da help n telin me bout da boox gurlu rok letz go shopin 2getha!

XXXXXXXXXXXXXXXXXX666XXXXXXXXXXXXXXXXXXXXXXXXXXXX

The door opened and Proffesor Rumbridge and Cornelia Fudge stomped out angrily. Then Dumbledum and Rumbridge sawed us.

"MR. WAY WHAT THE BEEP ARE YOU DOING!" Rumbridge shouted angrily. Dumbledore blared at her.

"Oops she made a mistake!" he corrupted her. "She means hi everybody cum in!"

Well we all came in angrily. So did all the other students. I sat between Darkness and Draco and opposite B'loody Mary. Crab and Goyle started 2 make some morbid jokes. They both looked exactly like Ville Vollo. I eight some Count Chocula and drank som blood from a cup. Then I herd someone shooting angrily. I looked behind me it was………Vampire! He and Draco were shooting at eachother.

"Vampire, Draco WTF?" I asked.

"You fucking bustard!" yelled Draco at Vampire. "I want to shit next to her!1"

"No I do!" shouted.

"No she doesn't fucking like u, you son of a bitch!" yelled Draco.

"No fuck you motherfucker she laves me not you!" shouted Vampire. And then……………… he jumped on Draco! (no not in dat way u perv) They started to fight and beat up each other.

Dumbldore yelled at them but they didn't stop. All of a sudden…… a

terrible man with red eyes and no nose flew in on his broomstick. He had no nose and was wearing a gray robe. All the glass in the window he flew thru fell apart. Britney that fucking prep started to cry. Vampire and Draco stopped fighting....I shopped eating....Everyone gasped. Da room fell silent....................Volzemort!

"Eboby.....Ebony......." Darth Valer sed evilly in his raspy voice. "Thou havfe failed ur mission. Now I shall kill thou and I shall kill Vampire as well. If thou does not kill him before then I shall kill Draco too!"

"Plz don't make me kill him plz!" I begged.

"No!" he laughed crudely. "Kill him, or I shall kill him anyway!" Then he flew away cackling.

I bust into tears. Draco and Vampire came to contort me. Suddenly my eyes rolled up so they looked all cool and gothic. I had a vision were I saw some lighting flash and then Voldremot coming to kill Draco while Draco slit his wrists in a depressed way.
"No!" I screamed sexily. Suddenly I locked up and stopped having the vision.

"Ebony Ebony aure you alright?" asked Draco in a worried voice.

"Yeah yeah." I said sadly as I got up.

"Everyfing's all right Enoby." said Vampire all sensetive.

"No its not!" I shouted angrily. Tearz of blood went down my face. "OMFG what if I'm getting possessed like in Da Ring 2!"

"Its ok gurl." said B'loody Mary. "Maybe u should ask Proffesor Sinister about what the visions mean though."

"Ok bich." I said sadly and den we went.

Chapter 24.

AN: prepz stup flaming da story ur jus jelous so fuk u ok go 2 hel!11 raven fagz 4 di help!

XXXXXXXXXXXXXXXXXXXXX666XXXXXXXXXXXXXXXX

Well we had Deviation next so I got to ask Proffessor Trevolry about the visions.

"Konnichiwa everybody come in." said Proffesor Sinister in Japanese. She smelled at me with her gothic black lipstick. She's da coolest fucking teacher ever. She had long dead black hair with blood red tips and red eyes. (hr mom woz a vampire. She's also haf Japanese so she speaks it and everyfing. she n b'loody mry get along grate) She's really young for a teacher. 2day she was wearing a black leather top with red lace and a long goffik black ripped dress. We went inside the black classroom with pastors of Emily the Strong. I raced my hand. I was wearing some black naie Polish with red pentagrams on it.

"What is it Ebony?" she asked. "Hey I love ur nail polish where'd u get it, Hot Topik?"

"Yeah." I answered. All the preps who didn't know what HT was gave me weird looks. I gave them the middle finger. "Well I have to talk to you about some fings. When do you want to due it?"

"Ho about now?" she asked.

"OK." I said.

"OK class fucking dismissed every1." Proffesor Trevolry said and she let every1 go. "Except for you Britney." she pointed at Britney and sum other preps. "Please do exorcize (geddit) 1 on page 3."

"OK I'm having lotz of visions." I said in a worried voice. I'm so worried is Draco gong 2 die.

Well she gave me a black cryptal ball to lock in. I looked at it.

"What do you c?" she asked.

"I said I see a black gothic skull and a pentagram."

Suddenly there was a knock at the door. I looked at it. It was Draco. He was looking really sexy wearing a black leather facet, a black gothic Linkin Park t-shirt and blak Congress shoes.

"Okay you can go now, see ya cunt." said Proffesor Sinister.

"Bye bitch." I said waving.

I went to Draco and Vampire was sitting next to him. We both followed Draco together and I was so exhibited.

Chapter 25.

AN: stop flaming ok if u dnot den il tel Justin 2 bet u up!1111 n il tel al da nredz 2 put vrtuz in ur computer!11111111111 FUK UU!1 raven fangz for de help!1

XXXXXXXXXXX666XXXXXXXXXXXXXXXX

I was so excited. I fellowed Draco wandering if we where going 2 do it again. We went outside and then we went into Draco's black car.

"Ebony what the fuck did Profesor Trevolry say." whispered Draco potting his gothic whit hand with bvlak nail polish on mine.

"She said she would tell me what the visions meant torromow." I grumbled in a sexy voice. He took out a heroin cabaret and spiked it, and gave it to me to spork. He started to fly the car into a tree. We went to the top of it. Draco put on some MCR.

"And all the things that you never ever told me
And all the smiles that are ever gonna haunt me." sang Gerard's sexy voice. We started tiling of each other's cloves fevently. He took of my blak thong and my black leather bar. I took of his black boxers.
Then......................... he put his trobbing you-know-what in my tool sexily.

"OMFG Draco Draco!" I screamed having an orgism. We stated frenching passively. Suddenly............ I fell asleep. I started having a dream. In it a black guy was shooting two goffik men with long black hair.

"No! Please don't fucking kill us!1" they pleaded but he just kept shooting them. He ran away in a red car.

"No! Oh my fucking god!11" I shouted in a scared voice.

"Ebony what's wrong?" Draco asked me as I woke up opening my icy blue eyes.

I started to cry and tears of blood went down my face. I told Draco to call Vampire. He did it with his blak Likin Park mobile. Butt the worst thing was who the ppl who were shot in the dream where........................... Lucian and Serious!111

Chapter 26.

AN: PREPZ STUP FLAMING SDA STRY OK!1 if u dnot lik da story den go fok urself u fokeng prep! U SUK!111 oh y and I wuznt beng rasist ok!11

XXXXXXXXXXXXXX666XXXXXXXXXXXXXXXXXX

A few mutates later Vampire came 2 da tree. He was wearing a blak leather jackson, black leather pants and a Good Chralotte t-shirt.

"Hi Vampire." I said flirtily as I started to sob. Draco hugged me sexily tryont to comfrot me. I started to cry tears of blood and then told them what happened.

"Oh fuck it!" Vampire shouted angrily. He4 started to cry sadly. "What fucking dick did that!"

"I don't know." I said. "Now come on we have 2 tell Dumbledor."

We ran out of the tree and in2 da castle. Dumblydor was sitting in his office.

"Sire are dads have been shot!" Draco said while we wipped sum tears from his white face. "Enoby had a vision in a dreem."

Dubleodre started to cockle. "Hahahaha! And How due u aspect me to know Ebony's not divisional?"

I glared at Dumbledore.

"Look motherfucker." he said angrily as Dumbeldore gasped *(c is da toot of crakter)*. "U know very well that I'm not decisional. Now get some fucking ppl out there to look for Series and Lucian- pornto!"

"Okay." he said in a intimated voice. "Were are they?"

I fought about it. Then all of a sudden..... "Longdon." I said. I told him

which street. He went and called some people and did some stuff. After a few mistunes he came back and said people were going out looking for them. After a while someone called him again. He said that they had been found. Draco, Vampire and I all left to our rooms together. I went with Draco to wait in the nurses office while Vampire went to slit his wrists in his room. We looked at each other's gothic, derperessed eyes. Then, we kissed. Suddenly Serious and Lucian came in on stretchers............................and Proffesor Sinister was behind them!1

Chapter 27. vampirz wil never hurt u

AN: u no wut!111 I dnot giv a fok wut u prepz fink abot me!1111 so stup

flaming da foking story bichez!1111 fangz 2 raven 4 ur luv n sport n help i luv u gurl soz i kodnt update lol I wuz rly deprezzd n I silt muh rists I had 2 go 2 da hospital rraven u rok gurl!11111111111111111111111

XXXXXXXXXXX666XXXXXXXXXXXXXXXXXXXXXXXXX

Every1 in the room stated to cry happly- I had saved them. Drako, Lucian, Serious bond Vampire all came to hug me. The nurse started to give them medicine.

"Cum on Enoby." said Proffesor Sinatra. She was wearing a gothic blak leader dress with a corset top and real vampir blood on it and fuking black platinum boots. "I have to tell you the fucking perdition."

I locked at Lucian, Serifs, Drake and Vampire. They nodded.

I smelled happily and went into a dark room. I had changed Profesor Sinister took out some black cards. She started to look into a black crucible ball. She said........................ "Tara, I see drak times are near." She said badly. She peered into da balls. "You see, you must go back in time." She took out a Time-Toner like B'loody Mary had. "When Voldemint was in Hogwarts before he became powerful he gut his hearth borken. Now do you fink he would still become Volxemort if he was in love?" I shook my head. "U must go back in time and sedouce him. It is the only way. If he is still evil then you must kill him. You can come to my room tomorrow and you can do it."

"Okay." I said sadly. We did dethz tuch sin. I went outside again sadly.

"What fucking happened?" asked Draco and Vampire.

"Yeah what happened?" asked Darkness, Willow and Boldy Mary?

I was about to tell them butt every1 was there. They were celebrating Lucian and Sirius being fond. Everyone was proud of me butt I jut

wonted 2 talk 2 Draco. They were cheesing my name and some reporters were there, trying to interview Dumblydore. A banner was put up. Lotz of fucking prepz were there oviously tring 2 be b goffik wering the HIM sign on their handz- depite them not having akshelly heard of him. Even Mr. Noris looked happy. A blak and red cake had been brought out. Crabbe and Goyke set up some fireworx in the shape of skulls from Wesley's Whizard Wises.

I put on my Invisibility coke with Vampire and Draco and we sneaked outside 2gether.

Chapter 28.

XXXXXXXXXXXXXXX666XXXXXXXXXXXXXXXXXXXXXXXX

We went in2 a blak room. The wallz were blak with portraits of gothic bands lik MCR, GC and Marlin Mason all over them. A big black coffin was in the middle. Red vevlet lined da blak box. There were three chairs made of bones with real skullz in dem. I wuz wearing a blak corset bar wif purple stuff on it, fishnet suckings and a blak leather thong underneath.

I sat down one of da chairs dispersedly. So did Drako and Vampire.

"Are you okay?" Vampir asked potting his albastard hand on mine. He was wearing black nail polish. I was wearing blak nail polish with red crosses on it.

"Yah I guess." I said sadly. Drako also pot his hand on mine sexily. I smiled sadly with my blak lipstick. "The problem is...........................I have to seduce Volxemort. Ill have 2 go bak in time"

Draco started to cry sadly. Vampire hugged him.

"Itz okay Eboby." he said finally. "But what about me? Ur not gonna brake up or anyfing, are you?"

"Of coarse not!" I gasped.

"Really?" he asked.

"Sure." I said.

We frenched sexily. Vampire looked at us longingly.

Then............ I took off Draco's MCR shrift and seductvely took of his pants. He was hung lik a stallone. He had replaced the Vampire tattoo that said Enoby on it. Black roses were around it. I gasped. He lookd exactly lik Gerard Way. Vampire took a vido camera. (I had sed it wuz ok b4).

I took of my clothes den we were in 4 da rid of r lif.

We started freching as we climbed into the cofin. He put his spock in my you-know-what and passively we did it.

"I love you Eboby. Oh let me feel u I need 2 feel u." he screamed as we got an orgasm. We watched Vampire filmed everything perfectly. Suddenly...........................

"WHAT THE FUCK R U DOING!"

It was............................Snope and Profesor McGoggle!111

Chapter 29.

AN: sot das fok up!11 ur jus jelouz koz ur prepz so fok u!1111 raven u rok gurl fangz 4 da help MCR ROX 666!111111111111

XXXXXXXXXXX666XXXXXXXXXXXXXXXXXXXXXXXXXXX

"Oh my satan!1" we screamed as we jamped out of da coffin. Snap and Professor McGoonagle started to shoot at us angrily.

"CUM NOW!1!" Preacher McGongel yielded. We did guiltily. We left the room putting on our clothes. Snoop garbed the caramel and put it in his pocket.

"Hey what the fuck!111" Vampire shooted angrily.

"Yeah buster what the fuck are u going to do with the fucking camera?" Draco demonded all protective, looking at me Longley with his gothic red eyes. "Look, Dumblehor noes your little secret and if u do dis again, then u will go to St Mango's. So give back da camera!1111"

Hahahaha the Mystery of Mogic thinks he is crazy there is no way dey wil believe him. Snoop laughed meanly.

"Yes so shut your mputh you inlosent fools!" yelled Proffesor McGoggle. She made us cum into a weird room with white stones all around it. There were all these werid tools in it. Draco started to cry all sexy and sexitive *(geddit koz hes a sexbom lol tom felnot rulez 4 lif but nut as muxh as gerard ur sex on legz I luv u u fokeng rok mary me!111).*

I started to cry tearz of blood *(it hapnz in vrampir kroniklz raven sed so ok so fok u!1).* Vampire took out a black honkerchief and started to wipe my red eyes.

And then.................. he and Snoop both took out guns using magic. They started to shoot each other angrily. Non of the ballots gut on eachodder yet. I took out my wand.

"Crosio!" I shouted. Snap stated 2 scram he dropd da gun. But it was too late. Both of them had run out of ballets. I STOPPED DA CURSE. Profesor McGoogle did a spell so that we were all chained up. She took out a box of tools. Den she said "OK Serverus I'm going 2 go now." She left. Snap started to laugh evilly. Vampire started to cry.

"It's ok Enoby." said Draco. "Evergreen will be all right. Remember the cideo u took of Snake."

Snape laughed again. And then...he took out some whips!1!1111

Chapter 30.

AN: stop flaming da story ok u dnot no wutz even gona happen ok!1111 so FUL U!111 if u flam u wil be a prep so al flamerz kan kiss muh ass!111 soz 4 soz 4 sayin alzhimers is dongerous but datz da mysteries opinin koz sosiety basically sux. fangz 2 raven u rok bich!111

XXXXXXXXXXXXX666XXXXXXXXXXXXXXX

"No!11" we screamed sadly. Snap stated loafing meanly. He took out a kamera anvilly. Then...................... he came tords Darko!1! He took sum stones out of his poket. He put da stones around Draco and nit a candle.

"What the fuck r u doing!" I shooted arngrily. Snoop laughed meanly. He polled down his pants. I gasped- there was a Dork Mark on his you-know-wut!11!

He waved his wand and a nife came. He gave da knife 2 me.

"U must stab Vrompire." he said to me. "If u don't then I'll rap Draco!1"

"No you fucking bastrad!1" I yielded.

But den Draco looked at me sadly with his evil goffik red eyes dat looked so depressant and sexy. He lookd exactly like a pentragram *(lol geddit koz im a satanist)* between Kurt Cobain and Gerard. But then I looked at Vampire and he looked so smexy too wif his goffik black hair. I thought of da time when we screwed and the time I did it with Draco and Dumblydore came and the tame where Draco almost commited suicide and Vampire wuz so sportive.

Snipe laughed angrily. He started to prey to Volxemort. He started to do an incapacitation dancing around the stokes whipping Draco and Vampire. Suddenly an idea I had. I clozd my eyes and using my vampire powers I sent a telepathetic massage to Drako and Vampire so they would destruct Snape.

"Dumbeldork will get u!" Draco shooted.

"Yah just wait ubtil da Mystery find out!11" Vampire yelled. Meanwhile I took out my wand.

"You ridiculus dondderhed!111" Snoop yielded. He took off all of Drico's clothes. Just as he was about to rape him……………………

"Crosio!" I shited pointing my wound. Snoop scremed and started running around da room screming. Meanwhile I grabed my blak mobile and sent a txt 2 Serious. I stopped doing crucio.

"You dunderhed!111 Im going to kill-" shooted Snape but suddenly Serverus came.

Snake put the whip behind his bak. "Oh hello Sev I wuz just teaching them sumthing." he lied. But suddenly Lusian and Profesor Trevolry came in2 da room and they and Serious unlocked the chains and put dem around Snap. Then Profesor Trevolry said 'Come on Ebony let's go."

Chapter 31.

AN: I sed shut da fok up u quiephs!111 stop kalin ebony a mary su ok u dnot even do no wutz gong 2 happen ok so fuk u!1111 fangz 2 muh bff raven 4 di help!1111

XXXXXXXXXXXXXX666XXXXXXXXXXXXXXXXX

"I always knew u were on Voldemort's side, you sun of a bitca *(bufy rox!111)*." Serious said 2 Snape.

"No I'm not I was teaching them somefing!1" Snap clamed.

"Oh fucking yeah?" I took some blak Volremortserum out of my poket and gave it to Serverus. He made Snap dirnk it. He did arngrily. Then Luscious took out a tape recorder and started playing it while he did curses on Snap. Then Proffesor Sinister and Lucian made us get out wif them while Snape told his secretes. Lucian took Vampure and Draco to the nurse after thanking me a millon times. Profesor Trevolry took me to a dark room. Now I wuz going to go back in time to sedouce Volxemort. Moving posters of MCR and Nrivana were all over. Hermoine, Darkness and Willow came too. B'loody Mary gave me a blak bag from Tom Rid's store.

"Whatz in da bag?" I asked Profesor Trevolry.

"U will c." she said. I opened thee bag. In it was a sexy tite low-smut black leather gothic dress. It had red korset stuff and there was a silt up da leg. I put it on. My frendz helped me put on blak fishnetz and blak pointy boots Willow had chosen. Willow and Darkness helped me put on black eyeliner and blod-red lipshtick.

"You look fucking kawaii, bitch." B'loody Mary said.

"Fangs." I said.

"Ok now you're going to go back in tim." said Proffesor Sinister. "U will have to do it in a few sessionz." She gave me a blak gun. I put it in a strap on my fishnetz like in Redisnet Evill. Then she gave me a black time-tuner. "After an hour use da time torner to go back here." Proffesor Trevolry said. Then she and B'loody Mary put a Pensive in front of me. Every1 went in front of it.

"Good luk!1" Everryone shooted. Darkess and Willow gave me deth's touch sin. Then........... I jumped sexily in2 da Pensive.

Suddenly I was in fornt of teh School. In front of me wuz one of da sexiest goth guyz I had ever seen. He was wering long blak hair, kinda like Mikey Way only black. He had gren eyes like Billie Joe Amstrung and pale whit skin. He wuz wearing a blak ripped up suit wif Vans. It was.......................Tom Bombodil!1111

Chapter 32.

AN: I sed stup fflaming I no his nam iznt tom bodil dat wuz a mistak!1111 if u dnot lik de story den u kan go skrew urself!11111 U SUK!111111

XXXXXXXXXXXXXXXXXX666XXXXXXXXXXXXX

"Hi." I said flirtily. "Im Enoby Way da new student." I shok my pale handz wif their blak noil polish wif him.

"Da name's Tom." he said. "But u kan call me Satan. Datz ma middle nam"

We shok hands. "Well come on we have 2 go upstairs." Satan said. I followed him. "Hey Satan........do u happen to be a fan of Gren Day?" *(sinz mcr and evinezenz dont exist yet den)* I asked.

"Oh my fuking god, how did u know?" Satan gasped. "actually I like gc a lot too."*(geddit coz gc did that song I just wanna live that's ounded really 80s)*

"omg me too!" I replied happily.

"guess what they have a concert in hogsment." satan whispered.

"hogsment?" I asked.

"yeah that's what they used to call it in these time before it became Hogsmeade in 2000." he told me all sekrtivly. "and theres a really cool shop called Hot-"

'topic!" I finshed, happy again.

He froned confusedly. "noo its called Hot Ishoo." He smiled skrtvli again. "then in 1998 dey changd it to hot topic." he moaned.

"ohh." now everything was making sense for me. "so is dumblydor your princepill?" I shouted.

"uh-huh." he looked at his black nails. "im in slitherin'"

"OMfG SHME TOO!" I SHRIEDKED.

"u go to this skull?" *(geddit cos im goffik)* he asked.

"yah that's why im here im NEW." I SMELLED HAPPili.

Suddenly dumblydore flew in on his broomstuck and started shredding at us angrily. "NO TALKING IN THE HALLS!" he had short blonde hair and was wearing a polo shirt from Amrikan ogle outfters. "STUPID GOFFS!"

satan rolled his eyes. "his so mean to us goffs and punks just becose we're in slytherine and we're not preps."

I turned around angrily. "actually I fink mebe its becos ur da barke lord."

"wtf?" he asked angrily.

"oh nuffin." I said sweetly.

then suddenlyn.................. the floor opened. "OMFG NO I SCEAMED AS I FEEL DOWN. everyone looked At ME weirdly."

"hey where r u goin?" satan asked as I fell.

I got out of the hole n it was bak in the pensive in professor trevolry's classroom. dumblydum wuz dere. "dumblydore I think I just met u." I said.

"oh yeah I rememba that." dumblydor said, trying to be all goffik.

sinister came in. "hey dis is my classroom wait wtf enoby what da hell r u doing?"

:"um." I looked at her.

"oh yeaH I forgot bout that."

"wth how?" I screamed forgetting she was a teacher for a second. but shes a goff so its ok.

professor sinster looked sad. "um I was drinking voldemortserum." she started to cry black tears of depression. dumblydum didn't know about them.

"hey r u crying tears of blood?" he asked curiously, tuching a tear.

"fuck off!" we both said and dumblydum took his hand away.

professor sinster started crying again in her chair, sobbing limpid tears. "omfg enoby...I think im addicted to Voldemortserum."

AN: SEE U FOKKING PREPZ GO FOK URSELXXZ DATZ SERUS ISSUZ 2O GO 2 HELL!1111112

Chapter 33.

AN: I sed shut up itz nut my folt ok if u don't lik da story den ur a prep so fuk u flamerz!1111 ps im nut updating ubtil u giv me fiv god reviewz nd diz tim I men it!111111 U SUK!1111 fangz raven 4 di help il promiz to help u wif ur story lolz1

XXXXXXXXXXXXX666XXXXXXXXXXXXX

"Oh my fuking god!1" I shooted sadly. "Shud we get u 2 St Manga's, bitch?"

"Hel no!" she said. "Lizzen Egogy, I need ur help. Nex tim u go bak in tim, do u fink u kod ask Tom Andorson 4 sum help?"

"Sure I said sadly. I went outside the door. Draco was there!111 He wuz wearing a big blak GC tshit which wuz his panamas.

"Hey Sexxy." I said.

"How'd it go Enoby?" he asked in his voice was so sexy and low kinda like Gerard Way when hes talking.

"Fine." I reponded. We stared 2 go bak in2 da dorm.

"How far did u go wif Satan?" Drako asked jealously.

"Not 2 far, lol." I borked.

"Will you hav to do it with him?" Draco asked angstily.

"I hop not 2 far!111" I shouted angrily. Den I felt bad 4 shooting at him. I said sorry. We frenched.

"What happened 2 Snipe?" I growled.

"U will see." Draco giggled mistressly. He opened a door..............Snap

nd Lumpkin werz there!11 Serious waz pokering dem by staging dem wif a blak nife.

"NOOOO PLZ!1111" Lumpkin bagged as Serious started 2 suk his blood. I laffed statistically. I tok some photons of him and Snap bing torqued. (ok I no dis iz men but fink abot it ppl dey r pedoz nd Snap trid 2 rap dem and neway sadiztz rok haz any1 seen shrak atak 3 lolz). We took sum of Snipe's blod den Drako and I went bak 2 our roomz. We sat on my goffik blak coffin. My cloves were kinda drity so I pot on a blak leather outfit fingie kinda like da 1 Suelene haz in Undreworld. (if u haven't herd of it den FUK U!111) . I put on some blak platform high heelz. Darko put on 'desolition liverz' by MCR.
Den..we storted 2 take of eachotherz clozez. I tok of his shit nd he had a six-pak, lolz. We started 2 mak out lik in Da Grudge. He pot his wetnes in my u-know-what sexily. I gut an orgy.

"Oh Draco!111111!1 Oh mi fuking gud Draco!1111" I screemed passively as he got an eructation.

"I luv u TaEbory." he whispred sexily and den we fel aspleep lol.

Chapter 34.

AN: SHOT DA FOK UP PREPZ!1111 hav u even red de story!11 u r proly al just prepz nd posrs so FUK U!111 fangz 2 raven 4 da help!1

XXXXXXXXXXXXXXXXXX666XXXXXXXXXX

I wook up in da coffin de next day. Draco waz gone. I got up and put on a blak tight sexah drsss that was all ripped at da end. There wuz red korset stuff going up da fornt and da bak and it came up 2 my knees. There wuz a slit in da dress lik in mr & mr simth. I pot on ripped blak fishnets and blak stilton bo-ots. Suddenly...................... Sorious cocked on da door. I hopened it.

"Hi Ibony." he said. "Gezz wut u have 2 cum 2 Profesor Sinistor's office."

"Ok." I said in a deprezzd voice. I had wanted to fuk Draco or maybe lessen to MCR or Evonezcence. I came anyway.

"So what the fuck happened 2 Snipe and Loopin?" I asked Sorious flirtily.

"I fucking tortured them." he answered in a statistic way. "They r in Abkhazian now, lol."

I laughed evilly.

"Where r Draco and Vampira?" I muttered.

"Dey are xcused form skool 2day." Sodomize moaned sexily. "Rite now they are watching Da Nigtmare b4 Xmas."

We went into da office. Proffesor Sinister was there. She was wearing a goffik blak dress that was all ripped all over it kinda lik da one Amy Lee wears in this pic

(http/ She wuz drinking some Volximortserum.

She took out da Pensiv and the time-torner.

"Enoby, you will have to do anozzer session now. Also I need u to get me da cure 4 being adikited." she said sadly. "Good luck. Fangz!"

And then..........I jumped into the Prinsive again. Suddenly I looked around..............I was in da Grate Hall eating Count Chorcula. It was mourning. I was sitting next to Satan. On a table was a tall gottik man wif long blak hair, pail skin and blue eyes wering a suit and blak Cronvrese shoes. He looked just like Charlyn Manson. I noticed......he was drinking a portent.

"Whose he!11" I asked.

"Oh, datz Profesor Slutborn." Satan said. "He's da Portents teacher.............Ebony?"

"Yah?" I asked.

"Did u know dat Marylin Mason is playing in Hogsemade tonight? And they r showing The Exercise at da movies b4 dat."

"Yah?"

"Well......want 2 go 2 da contort and da movie wif me?"

Chapter 35. gost of u

AN: *fangz 2 suzi 4 da idea!1 u rok! fuk of prepz!11111111 fangz 2 raven 4 di help u rok gurl!1 ps im gong 2 end da stroy rlly sun so FUK U!111 oh yah nd if u no eny gofik namz plz tel me koz I ned 1 4 serius!1 fangz.*

XXXXXXXXXXXXXXXXXXXX666XXXXXXXXXXXXXXXXXXXX

I went in2 da Conmen Room finking of Satan. Suddenly I gasped..................Draco wuz there!111

I grasped. He locked as hut as eva werring blak ledder pants, a blak Lonken Prak t-shrit and blak eyeliner.

"Draco what da fuk r u dong!111111" I gosped.

"Huh?" he asked. Then I remembred. It wuzn't Draco. It was Lucan!1 He stil had two arms.

"Oh hi Lucian!1" I sed. "Im Ebony the new student lol we shook handz."

"Yah Satan told me abot you." Lusian said. He pinted to a groop of sexxxy gottik guyz. They where siting in a corner kutting. It wuz Serious, Vampire's dad and..................Snap! All of them were wearing blak eyeliner and blak Good Chralootte band shirts. "Lizzen I'm in a goth band wif those guys." he said. "Were playing 2nite at da Marylin Mason show as back-up.

"ORLY." I ESKED.

"Yeah." he said. "Were calld XBlakXTearX. I play teh gutter. Spartacus plays da drums" he said ponting to him. "Snap plays the boss. And Jamez plays the guitar to even fo we call him Samaro, after Samara in da ring."

"Hey bastards." I told them they gave me Dethz tuch sin. Suddenly I gasped again. "But don't u have a lead singer!" I asked. Lucian looked dawn sadly.

"We uzd to but she did. She contempted suicide by silting her rists."

"Oh my fuking god!11 Datz so fuking sad!1" I gasped.

"Its okay but we need a new led snigger." Samaro said.

"Wel..........I said Im in a bnad myself."

"Rilly?" asked Snap. I cudnt belive it. He used 2 b goffik!111

"Yeah were called Blody Gothik Rose 666. Do u wanna hr me sing?"

Yeah said everyone. So the guys tok out der guitarz. They began to pay a song bi *(geddit koz bi guyz r sooo sexah!11)* Gurn Day.

"I wok dis empt stret on da bolevrad of broken dremz." I sang sexily *(I dnot own da lyrikz 2 dat song)*.. Every1 gasped.

"Enopby? Will u join da band? Plz!1" begged Lucian, Samoro, Serious and Snap.

"Um........ok." I shrugged. "Are we gong to play tonight?"

"Yah." they said.

"Ok." I said but I new dat I had 2 get a new outfit. I walked outside wondering how I kud go forward in time. Suddenly someone jumped in fornt of me. It wuz.....Morty Mcfli!1 He was wering a blak bnad tshrit and blak bagy jeans.

"What da hell r u dong here!11" I asked.

"I wil help u go frowad in tim Enoby." he said siriusly Den..........he took out a blak tim machine. I went in2 it and.........................sudenly I wuz forward in tim!111

Chapter 36.

AN: I sed stop flaming ok!111111111 I bet u r al proly old srevinty yr oldz!111 ps PORTERSUZ UR A PREP!1 o ya nd fangz 2 raven 4 di help!111 hav fun in englond gurl!11111

XXXXXXXXXXXXXXXXX666XXXXXXXXXXXXXXXXXXXX

I loked around in a depresed way. Suddenly I saw Profesor Sinister. B'lody Mary, Socrates and Draco, Vampire and Willow were their to.

"OMFG Sorius I saw u nd Samaro and Snip nd everyone!11111 I kant beleev Snap uzd 2 b goffik!111111"

"Yah I no." Serious said sadly.

"Oh hey there bitch." Profesor Trevolry said in an emo voice dirnking some Volxemortserom.

Hi fuker." I said. "Lizzen, Satan asked me out to a gottik cornet and a movie so I need a sexah new outfit for da date. Also I'm playng in a gothic band so I need an ootfit for that too."

"Oh my satan!1" (geddit lolz koz shes gofik) gasped B'lody Mary. "Want 2 go to Hot Topik to shop 4 ur outfit?"

"OMFS, letz have a groop kutting session!11" said Profesor Trevolry.

"I can't fucking wait 4 dat but we need 2 get sum stuff first." said Willow.

"Yah we need sum portions for Profesor Trevolry so she wont be adikted 2 Volxemortserum anymore nd also............sum luv potion 4 Enoby." Darko said resultantly.

"Well we have potions klass now." Willow said so let's go.

We went sexily to Potionz class. But Snap wasn't there. Instead there was……………………………………Cornelio Fuck!11111

"Hey where the fuck is Dumblydore!111" Draco shouted angrily.

"STFU!1" shooted Cornelia Fuck. "He is in Azkhabian now wif Snip and Loopin he is old and week he has kancer. "Now do ur work!111"

My friendz and I talked arngrily.

"Can you BELEVE Snap used to be gottik!1" Vampire asked surprisedly.

"DATZ IT!11" CORNELIO FUK SHOOTED ARNGRILY. "IM GETTING PROFESOR BRIDGE!111"

He stomped out angrily.

Mi frendz and I began talking again. I began to drink some blod mixed wif beer. Suddenly I saw Hargrid in da cupboard.

"WTF is he doing?" I asked. Then I looked at Draco. He wuz wearing tonz of eyeliner nd he locked shexier den eva. Suddenly……………"HARGRIF WUT DA FOK R U DOING!11" he shooted.

I looked around……………Hairgrid wuz putting sumfing in my glass of blod!11 Darko and Vampire started 2 beat him up sexily.

"God u r such a posr!1" I shooted at Hairgrid. Suddenly I looked ar what he was putting in da blood. It was………………Amnesia Portion!111

Chapter 37.

AN: OK EVRYBODY IM GONG ON VOCATION ON DA FRIST OF JULY SO IM EEDER GONNA END DA FIK OR UPDAT IT IN WEEX. fangz!1 oh yah nd prepz stop flaming sa story!11 raven fangz 4 da help c ya gurl afta vocation!11

XXXXXXXXXXXXXXX666XXXXXXXXXXXXXXXX

DARKO'S PONT OF VIEW LOL

Vampire and I chaind Hairgrid 2 da floor.

"Oh mi fucking satan!11" Enoby said. She wuz so hot. "Maybe I cud uze Amnesia potion 2 make Satan foll in love wif me faster!1"

"But u r so sexy and wonderful aneway Tata," said Vampire. "Why would u need it?"

"To make everyfing go faster lol." said Enoby.

"But you wont have to do it wif him or anyfing, will u?" I asked jelosly.

"OMFG u guyz r so scary!11" said Britney, a fucking prep.

"Shut the fuk up!1" said Willow.

"Ok well anyway lets go 2 Profesor Trevolry's room."

Draco, Ebory and I went to Profesor Siniater's room. But Profesor Sinister wasn't there. Instead Tom Rid was.

Oh hi fuckers he said. Lizzen, I got u sum kewl new clovez.

I took out da cloves from da bag. It was a goffik blak leather miniskirt that said '666' on da bak, black stilton bootz, blood red fishnetz and a

blak corset.

"OMG fangz!" I said hugging him in a gothic way. I took da clothes in da bag.

"OK Profesor Sinister isnt hr what the fuk should we do?" asked Draco. Suddenly he loked at a sign on da blak wall.

"Oh my fuking satan!1" I screamed as I read it. On it said Evry1 Profesor Sinister is away. She is too gottik she is in Azkhabian now. Classes shal be taught by Dubledork who is bak but he shall not be principal 4 now. Sincerely Profesor Rumbridge.

"OMFG!111" I shoted arngrily. "How could they do that!11"

Suddenly Dumblydore came.

"WHAT DA HELL R U DONG IN MY OFICE!1" he began to shoot angrily. Sudwenly I saw Morty Mcfly's blak tim machine!111 I jumped seductivly in2 it leaving Draco and Vampire. Sudenly I wuz back in tim!11 I looked around. It was..............Profesor Slutborn's efface! I sneaked around. Suddenly I saw da Amnesia potion on his desk. It wuz blak wif blood-red pentagramz in it. It was the shape of a cross. I put it in my poket. Suddenly da door opened it wuz........Profesor Slutgorn!11

OMG wut r u doing fuker he shooted angrily I don't kno wut da fuk r u DOING I SHOUTED ANGRILY.

"Oh sorry I wuz just looking around koz I thought it wuz class." you said finally hoping he couldn't c da potion in ur pocket.

"Oh ok u can go now." said Profesor Slutborn.

You went to the conmen room after putting on my clothes. Silas, Samaro and Snap were there practicing Vampirez will Never Hurt U by

MCR.

"Oh hi you guys." I said seductively. "Wheres Satan?"

"Oh he's cumming." said Serious. "BTW u can kall me Hades now."
Suddenly Satan came. He was wearing a smexxy blak leather Jackson,
blak congres shoes, a Slipnot t-shirt and a blak tie.

"Ok I will see you guyz at da concert." I said and then I went with Satan.

Chapter 38.

AN: wut doez every1 fink if I end da strory and den I add sum more 2 it after vocation? oh yah asnd prepz stup flaming if u dnot lik dat story den take muh quiz ok den u wil c if ur gofik or not!1111111

XXXXXXXXXXXXXXXX6666XXXXXXXXXXXXXXXXXX

Satan and I walked 2 his car. It wuz a blak car wif pentagrams all over it. On da license plate said 666 just lik Draco's car. I went in it seduktivly. Stan started 2 drive it. We talked about Satanism (lolz he wuz named after Satan), kuttting, musik and being goffik.

"Oh my satan, Gerard is so fuking hot!11" Volxemort agreed as we smoked sum weed. *(koz bi guyz r hot dey r so sensitive I luv dem lol goez fux a bi guy)*

"Lol, I totally decided not 2 comit suicide when I herd Hilena." I said in a flirty voice. "……….Hey Satan do u know da cure 4 when ppl r adikted 2 Volxemortseruem?"

"Well……………." he thought. "I fink u have 2 drink Vampire blod."

Suddenly Volxemort parked da car behind a blak movie theater. Satan and I walked outside. We went in2 da movie tether were they were showing da Excercist. In it a boy and a gurl were doing it sudenly a cereal killer came lol. Satan and I laughed at da blood koz we're sadists.

While Satan was watching da movie, I had an idea. I took Satan's gothic blak Nightmare b4 Christmas cigar sexily from his poket and put sum Amnesia potion in it. I put it bak in his blak Emile the Strange bag. Satan turned arund and started 2 smoke it. Blak cloudz wif red pentagramz ind em started 2 fly around everywhere.

"OMG!111" Satan said jumping up. I gasped koz I wuz afraid hed notizd. "Enoby gess what?"

I new that the amnesia had worked.

"Amnesia potion has not been invented yet so it will not work." He said. "2 badd coz I wanted 2 use sum on u."

"Kul." I raised my eye suggestingly. And den………. he tok of my cloves sexily and we started 2 make out. I tok of his shit. He had six-pak justr lik Gerard Way!11 We frenched.

"Xcuze me but u r going 2 have 2 leave!111" shooted da lady behind us she was a prep.

"Fuk u!11" I said. Suddenly………………… I attaked her suking all her blood.

"Noooooo!11" she screamed. All the preps in da theater screamed but everyone else crapped koz Satan and I loked so cute 2gether. Satan and I started to walk outside.

"Zomg how did u do that?" Voldremort asked in a turned-on voice.

"I'm a vampire." I said as we went into the car.

"Siriusly?" he gasped.

"Yah siriusly." I said drinking sum beer. Satan started 2 drive da car. I smelled happily.

"Itz too bad we didn't get 2 c da rest of the movie, don't u fink?"

"Yah." I said as we kised passively. Satan parked in a blak driveway next 2 da place where Draco and I had watched GC for the frist time. We went inside where Marylin Mason wuz playing and started to mosh lol.

"Anti-ppl now uve gone 2 far Jeus Krist Superstar!1111" screamed Marlin on da stage. We did the devil fingers. I started 2 dance really close to Satan. He was so shmexay!1 He looked at me all emo with his gothic red eyes and he looked exactly like Mikey Way. I almost got an orgaism!1 Suddenly Marylin Mason stopped singing.

"I wood like to peasant...............XBlakXTearX!11" he said. I ran onstage. Lucian, Samaro, Snap and Hades were there. They started 2 play their instilments. I got onstag.

"Wel if u wonted honesty datz all u had 2 say!1111" I sang. *(I dnot own da lyerix 2 dat song)* My voice sounded lik a pentagram betwen Amy Lee and a gurl version of Gerard Woy. Everyone clappd. Satan got an eructation. "I'M NUT OKAY!1" I sang finaly. Suddenly Lucian started playing da song wrong by mistak.

"OMFG!1" yielded James. "Wut the fuck?"

"Woops im sory!" said Lucian.

"You fuking ashhole!1" James shouted angrily.

"U guys are such prepz!11" Snap said. "Cum on it wuz a mistake!1"

"Yah itz not his fault!11" said Serious.

"No he ruined the fucking song!1" yelled Samaro.

"U guys stop!11" I shotoed angrily but it waz 2 late. They all began 2 fight. Sudenly Samaro took out hiz nife.

"OMFG no!11" shouted Lucan but it wuz 2 late James tried 2 shoot off his arm.

And den...........................I jumped secxily in front of da bullet!11

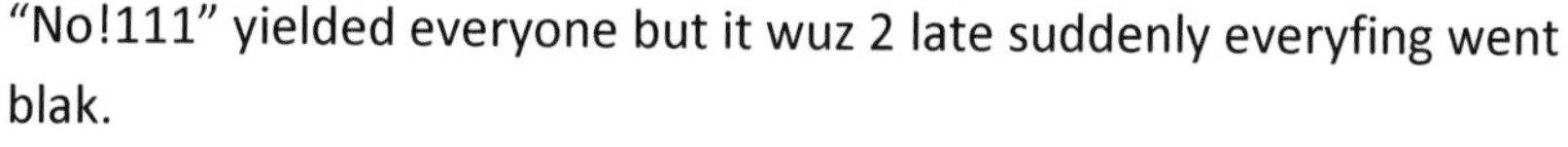

"No!111" yielded everyone but it wuz 2 late suddenly everyfing went blak.

Chapter 39. I Am A Trolling Genious, lolz

Disclaimer: I do not own the HP series and I am not the real
XXXbloodyrists666XXX.

AN// I am an extremely immature pathetic idiot girl, I know. Out of boredom, I
crack this girl's passy for fun (and it took less than 8 minutes to do it too) and
will probably get in a shitload of trouble. Which I probably deserve 'cause I'm
being a troll right now. Meh.

And I present to you MY crappy part in this story. (And take note I haven't even
finished reading this fic yet, but instead skip over to skim chapter 38.) Flame,
laugh, do whatever you want "preps."

I, the American retail wearing british vampire Sue, coughed up blood.

Satan kneeled down beside me.

"Nooooooooooooooooo! Don't die!"

I gave him a rueful smile. "I'm sorry. It's something I had to do, to fufill
my duty as the noble gothic Mary Sue."

Satan sobbed. "I love you Ebony."

"I love you two. I'll...I'll see you in hell." I mumbled, already finding my
surroundings fading to black.

B'loody Mary Smith suddenly popped into the room for no apparent
reason. She frowned when she realized the room was oddly quiet, but
at the sight of Ebony's lifeless body, she screamed. Her face became
pale with horror. She screamed for the healers, Dumbledore, Mcgoogle,
and every single gothic person she could think of.

Suddenly, a glow started to surround the body of Ebony. Everyone
stared in shock. Her body started to lift ever so slowly and then, to
everyone's shock, it started to incinerate.

When everyone realized what was happening, they rushed over to try to rescue the body, but it was too late, the Sue became nothing more then a pile of ashes.

A loud resounding of everyone bellowing
"NOOOOOOOOOOOOOOOOOOOOOO...!!" filled the room.

A flash of white light from the ashes then started to bounce around the room. Everyone cowered in fear and were temporarily blinded. When it was all over, things changed.

All the silly goth clothes dropped from everyone's bodies *(AN//I will refuse to explain how the hell that happened.)* and, in their place, clothes the characters would normally wear in canon appeared on their bodies.

When everyone got over the shock of becoming free of the gofick power, everybody cheered. Everyone started singing 'Ding dong the sue is dead...' Well, that is, until all the HP characters realized the true implications of becoming more canon like again.

All the characters who were supposed to be dead fell to the floor, their bodies cold and lifeless. Harry and Voldemort started dueling. On the left side of the two, the battle of the Light Side and the Dark Side were reaching a climax.

And, because the replacement author also likes to screw around with canon, Draco and Hermione fled the scene and got married.

Meanwhile...

Down in hell, Ebony shed a single tear because of her current situation. A situation that would live on for all eternity. Or at least until the end of fanfiction time.

She lost it all, but she knew she had to remain strong. Nothing would

ever break her down.

She looked down over her pale body, and frowned. 'Where are my emo clothes?' She asked herself in confusion.

And then it occured to her...

For her shirt, she was wearing a bright pink polo with a little seagull on the (right or left? I can't remember) side. Below that, she was wearing a denim miniskirt with the "destroyed" look on it. Paired underneath that skirt were leggings with a little moose at the bottom. And then Ebony realized, on her shoulder, she was carrying a pretty bag with an eagle on it that said Live Your Life written all over the bag.

Ebony supressed the urge to scream. Here she was decked out in clothes prep to the extreme wearing stuff from Abercrombie and Fitch, American Eagle, AND Hollister.

Panicked, Ebony hastily tried to take off the Hollister polo, but underneath it, there was another Hollister polo underneath. Ebony frowned, and looked under her shirt. All she saw was a bra underneath (dare I point out it's from the Aerie line available at American Eagle?). Ebony tried to remove the shirt again. But to her frustration, there was yet again another polo to replace it.

"THIS IS UNLOGICAL AND DOES NOT MAKE ANY SENSE!!" Ebony bellowed out to the air. She failed to see the irony in her statement, how hypocrytical her words were, seeing as she was practically calling the kettle black here.

Ebony slit her writs and mumbled to herself, "Omigod."

/End Crap Fic.

AN// Oh yeah, if you wanna see the original content this chick had planned for

this chapter, I accessed it through the document manager thingy, which I copied and pasted, so you can read it here:

AN: stfu prepz git a lif!111111 U SUCK!11 oh and form now on il be in vocation in englind until lik august so I wont be able 2 update 4 a while, lolz. fangz 2 evry1 hu revoiwed expect da prepz hu flamed FOK U!1 MCR RULEZ 666!111

XXXXXXXXXXXXXXXXXX666XXXXXXXXXXXXX

I woke up in da Norse's offace on a special gothik coffin. Hairgrid wuz in da bed opposite me in a comma coz Vampir and Draco had bet him up. Mr. Noris was cleaning the room.

"Oh mi satan wut happened!" I screamed. Suddenly Volxemort came. He loked less mean then usual.

"Get the fuk out u fucking bastard!11" I yielded.

"Thou hath nut killd Vampire yet!11" he said arngrily. Sudenly he started 2 cry tearz of blood al selective.

"Volxemort? OMFG what's wrong!111" I asked.

Sudenly.......... Lucian, Profesor Sinister and Serious came! B'lody Mary and Vampire were wif dem. Every1 was holding blak boxez. VOLXEMORT DISAPAERD.

"OMFG Enoby ur alive!111" Scremed Vampire. I hugged him and B'lody Mary.

"What the fuk happened?" I asked dem. "Oh my satan!11 Am I lik dead now?" I gosped.

"Enoby u were almost shot!11" said Serious. "But da ballet could not kill u since u were form anodder time."

"But fangz anyway!1" said Lucian holding oot his arm. I gasped. He had two arms!

"OMG I cant beleve Vampirz' dad shot u!1" I gasped.

"Well 2 be honest Snap wuz pozzesd by Snap bak den." said James.

"Yah he wuz a spy." Serious said sadly. "He wuz really a Death Dealer."

"And he wuz such a fuking poser 2!11" said Lucian. "He didn't even realy no hu GC were until I told him." Well anyway everyone tarted 2 give me presents. I was opening a blak box wif red 666s (there wuz a dvd of corps bride in it) on it when I gasped. Mr. Noris looked up angrily coz he h8ed gothz.

"Hey haz aneone fuking seen Draco?" I asked gothikally.

"No Draco told me he wood be watching Hoes of Wax." said Profesor Trevolry. "He duzzn't know dat ur better. Anyway da norse said u could get up. Cum on!1"

I got up suicidally. Lucian, Serious and Profesor Sinister left. I wuz wearing a blak leather nightgun. Under that I had on a sexxy blak leather bra trimed wif blak lace, with a matching thong that said goffik gurl on the butt and sexy fishnetz that kind hooked on 2 my thong (if u don't get da idea massage me ill tell u). I put on a blak fishnet top under a blak MCR t-shirt, a blak leather mini with blak lace and congress shoes. I left the hospital's wings wif B'lody Mary, Willow and Vampire.

"OMFG letz celebrate!11" gasped Willow.

"We can go c Hose of Wax wif Draco!1" giggled Vampire.

"Letz go lizzen 2 GC and kut ourselvz 666!11" said Hermoine. We opened da conmen room door sexily. And den..........I

gasped.................................... Draco wuz there doing it wif Snap!1111111111111111111111111 He wuz wearing a blak tshirt wif 666 on da front and baggy jeanz.

"U fucking prep!11" we all yielded angrily.

"Yah u betrayed us!111" shooted Vampire angrily as he took out his blak gun.

"No u don't understand!1" screamed Draco sadly as he took his thingie out of Snake's.

"No shit u fuking suk u preppy bastard!111" said Willow trying 2 attak him (u rok girl!1). I ran suicidally to my room I sexily took a steak out.

"Enoby no!11111" screamed Draco but it wuz 2 l8 I had slit muh ritsts wif it suddenly everyfing went blak again.

Sincerely,

An-Anon-Author-Who-Will-Silently-Not-Reveal-Her-Identity-Because-She's-A-Coward :P

A.K.A. Just a troll with rocks for brains.

Chapter 40. LOL! Someone has taken my account over!

THE IDIOT'S NOTE: Well... this was in the doc area... might as well let the whole world see what the real Tara wanted to show us... Have a nice day!

AN: stfu prepz git a lif!111111 U SUCK!11 oh and form now on il be in vocation in englind until lik august so I wont be able 2 update 4 a while, lolz. fangz 2 evry1 hu revoiwed expect da prepz hu flamed FOK U!1 MCR RULEZ 666!111

XXXXXXXXXXXXXXXXXXX666XXXXXXXXXXXX

I woke up in da Norse's offace on a special gothik coffin. Hairgrid wuz in da bed opposite me in a comma coz Vampir and Draco had bet him up. Mr. Noris was cleaning the room.

"Oh mi satan wut happened!" I screamed. Suddenly Volxemort came. He loked less mean then usual.

"Get the fuk out u fucking bastard!11" I yielded.

"Thou hath nut killd Vampire yet!11" he said arngrily. Sudenly he started 2 cry tearz of blood al selective.

"Volxemort? OMFG what's wrong!111" I asked.

Sudenly.......... Lucian, Profesor Sinister and Serious came! B'lody Mary and Vampire were wif dem. Every1 was holding blak boxez. VOLXEMORT DISAPAERD.

"OMFG Enoby ur alive!111" Scremed Vampire. I hugged him and B'lody Mary.

"What the fuk happened?" I asked dem. "Oh my satan!11 Am I lik dead now?" I gosped.

"Enoby u were almost shot!11" said Serious. "But da ballet could not kill u since u were form anodder time."

"But fangz anyway!1" said Lucian holding oot his arm. I gasped. He had

two arms!

"OMG I cant beleve Vampirz' dad shot u!1" I gasped.

"Well 2 be honest Snap wuz pozzesd by Snap bak den." said James.

"Yah he wuz a spy." Serious said sadly. "He wuz really a Death Dealer."

"And he wuz such a fuking poser 2!11" said Lucian. "He didn't even realy no hu GC were until I told him." Well anyway everyone tarted 2 give me presents. I was opening a blak box wif red 666s (there wuz a dvd of corps bride in it) on it when I gasped. Mr. Noris looked up angrily coz he h8ed gothz.

"Hey haz aneone fuking seen Draco?" I asked gothikally.

"No Draco told me he wood be watching Hoes of Wax." said Profesor Trevolry. "He duzzn't know dat ur better. Anyway da norse said u could get up. Cum on!1"
I got up suicidally. Lucian, Serious and Profesor Sinister left. I wuz wearing a blak leather nightgun. Under that I had on a sexxy blak leather bra trimed wif blak lace, with a matching thong that said goffik gurl on the butt and sexy fishnetz that kind hooked on 2 my thong (if u don't get da idea massage me ill tell u). I put on a blak fishnet top under a blak MCR t-shirt, a blak leather mini with blak lace and congress shoes. I left the hospital's wings wif B'lody Mary, Willow and Vampire.

"OMFG letz celebrate!11" gasped Willow.

"We can go c Hose of Wax wif Draco!1" giggled Vampire.

"Letz go lizzen 2 GC and kut ourselvz 666!11" said Hermoine. We opened da conmen room door sexily. And den...........I gasped............................... Draco wuz there doing it wif Snap!11111111111111111111111111111 He wuz wearing a blak tshirt wif

666 on da front and baggy jeanz.

"U fucking prep!11" we all yielded angrily.

"Yah u betrayed us!111" shooted Vampire angrily as he took out his blak gun.

"No u don't understand!1" screamed Draco sadly as he took his thingie out of Snake's.

"No shit u fuking suk u preppy bastard!111" said Willow trying 2 attak him (u rok girl!1). I ran suicidally to my room I sexily took a steak out.

"Enoby no!11111" screamed Draco but it wuz 2 l8 I had slit muh ritsts wif it suddenly everyfing went blak again.

Idiot's Note: Ugh... I know... terrible... but then again, this wouldn't be called the 'worst fanfic ever if not for the fact that the writing standards meets the level of a day old fetus...

Chapter 41.

AN: 2 every1 hu kepz flaming diz GIT S LIF!!!!! I bet u proly odnt no hu gerod way is ur proly al prepz and pozers!!!!!!!!11111 neway sum1 hakked in2 mi akkount in November and dey put up my last chaptah but now der is a new 1.

im surry 4 nut updating g 4 a while but ive been rilly bizzy. im trying 2 finish da story b4 da new movie kumz out. Im gong on vacation 4 a mons I wont be bak until abott 2 weeks. OMFG drako iz so hot in all da pix 4 da new movie!!!111 I wunted dem 2 put a kameo by geord way lol he hsud play drako. if u flame ill slit muh risztz!!!!!!!!!11 raven u rok gurl hav fun in ingland.

XXXXXXXXXXXXX666XXXXXXXXXXXXXXXXXX

When I wook up I wuz in a strange room. I loked around I wuz wearing da same outfit I had when is performed wif XBlakXTearX!!!!!11 I looked arund confusedly. It wuz da Norse's office but it looked difrent!! On da wall wuz a pik of Marlyin Munzon!!!1111 *(just imagin dat he is an 80s goffik band 2 ok koz he is more old den panic?! at da dizcko or mcr)* der wuz also a goffik blak Beatles calander with a picture of the beetlez werring iyeliner and blak cloves. On it said '1980.'

"OMFG!!! Im back in Tim again!!!!111" I screamed loudly. Suddenly Satan(dis is actually voldimort 4 photo refrenss!). Voldimort wuz wearing a blak leather Jackson, blak tight jeans and fishnet pantz. He looked so sexah I almost had an orgy!!!!11

"OMFG Enoby r u ok." He asked gothikally.

"Yah Im okay 4 ur in4mation." I snapped sexily. "OMG am I dedd???" koz I remembered I had jumped in front off da bullet from Jame's gun. I also rememberd cing Drako doing it wif Snap!!!!111

I guessed dat when I had slit mi wrists I had went bak in tim instead of dieing. I knoew I could go forward in time if I found a time-toner or da tim machine.

"No ur not dead." Satan reassured suicidally as he smokd a cigarette sexily and smoke came all over his face. "Ur a vampire so u kant die frum a bullet. Cum on now lets go c how Hairy's dad is doing."

I noo dat da real reason I didn't die from da ballet was koz I was from da future. "WTF!!!! James almust shot Luciious!!!" I said indigoally. I knew that James had really ben possezzed, but I didn't want him2 know I knew.

"Yah I know but he had a headache he wz under a lot of stress." Satan reasoned evilly.

"I guess that's ok." I said because James hadn't really shot Lucian. Also I noo that Lucian wood now have 2 arms instead of 1. I walked seduktivly outside with Satan. Suddeni I saw a totally sexi goffik bi guy!!!!!11 He had bleched blond hair wiv blak streaks up 2 his ears and he wuz wearing goffik blak iliner, a blak Green Day shirt (it showed billy joel wiv bolnd hair since it was da eighties), blak congress shoes and black baggy pants. He walked in all sexly like Gerrd way in the vido for I Don't 3 u lyk I did yesterday and you cud see a blak tear on his face lyk da wmn in dat video. "Hey." He sed all qwietly and goffically.

"Who da fuck is that?" I asked angrly cos I did nut kno him.

"Dis is...Hedwig!!!!!!!!!11" Sed Volximort. "He used to be in XBlackXTearX 2 but he had 2 dropp out koz he broke his arm.

"Hey Hedwig." I said seductively evn tho I wuz nut tring to b.

"Lol hi Enoby." He answered but then he ran away bcos he had hair of magical creature. He was humming Welcum 2 da Blak Prade under his breth(*I no dat is not 80s but pretend it is ok!!)*

"Bye." I sed all sexily.

"Dat was Hedwig. He used 2 b my boifreind but we broke up." Satan said sadly, luking at his blak nails.

"OMFG I can get u bak 2gether!" I said fingering something I didn't

know wuz in my pocket- a blak Kute is What we Aim 4 cideo ipod that I could take videos wif *(duz ne1 elze no about dem??? dey kik azz!!!!).*

"Ok u can 4get about ur class for now, Hedwig. Im going 2 show u something grate!!!!1" I led them to da Great Hall. "Cum on u guys."

Lucian, James, Serious and Snake were all in da Grate Hall. Lucian woudnt talk wiv James because he had tried 2 shoot him.

"Go fuk urself you fukking douche!" he shouted at him. "Drako is never gong 2 b frends with vampire now!!1"

"Yah go fuck urself Samaro!" Snape agreed but I noo he wuz lying koz it had been his folt James had almost shot Lucian.

"B quiet u guys." I said sexily. Mi plan waz working oot great. Now I kood make Voldement good wivout doing it with him! Now Vampire's dad wood never die and "OK Satan and Hedwig, u guys can start making out." I said and I started 2 film dem wiv da ipod.

"Kool." said Serious as Voldemort and Hedwig started 2 make out sexily. We watched as tdey started 2 take each odderz cloves off sexily. Samaro, Serious, Snake and Lucian all watched koz dey wer prolly bi. I noo Snape was bi.

"Oh my fukking god!!!! Voldimort! Voldimort!" screamed Hedwig as his glock touched Voldemort's.

But suddenly everything stopped as da door opend and in kame.................Dumblydore and Mr. Norris!!!!111111111111

Chapter 42. da blak parade

AN: omg da new book iz kumming out rlly soon I kant wait!!!1111. I fink dat snap will be really the same person as Volximort koz dey are both haff-blood so dat will explain y he kild dumblydore and he hated hairy!!!!!1111 nd den hairy wil have 2 kommit suicide so voldimort will die koz he will rilly be a horcrox!!!!!111 omg I hope draco nd harry get 2getha dat will be so shmexxy,

wont it?? If dey don't den JKR is hamophobic!!!!!111111 fangz 4 da help wiv facts, medusa u rok!!!111

XXXXXXXXXXXXXXX666XXXXXXXXXXXXXXXXXXXXXXXXX

I sat depressedly in Dumbledork's office wiv Hedwig, Satan, James, Serious, Snap and Lucian. Dumbledore was sitting in front of us cruelly. He looked more young den he did in da future. He had taken da ipod away and wuz now lizzening 2 a shitty Avril Levine song.

"What da hell is this anyway??" he cackled meanly. I hoped he didn't find out dat I was frum another time.

"Whatever u do don't blame Ibony, u jerk." Satan said.

"Yah, siriusly she was trying to get Satan and Hedwig back together." Serious said deviantly.

"Be quiet you Satanists." Dumbledore cockled. "If ur lucky I'll probably send u all to Akazaban!!! That will teach u to copolate in da Great Hall." He changed the song on da ipod 2 a n'Sync song. Suddenly I noticed sumfing strong about da Ipod. It was slowly chonging! Dumblydore didn't notece.

"You fucking poser." I muttoned.

"I bet you've never herd of GC." James said. Know I knew waht da iPod was chonging in2- Morti McFly's tim machine!!!!!11

"Shut up Jomes!!!" Drako's dad shouted.

"Yeah shut up!!!!" Snake said preppily.

"No u shut up Dumblydore!!!!!!!!1111" said Tom.

"I've had enough of u Satanists in my school!!!!" shouted Dumbledore spuriously.

Suddenly I grabed da iPod from him. "Evry1! Jump in b4 itz 2 l8!!! I jumped in2 it. But only 1 odder person jumpd in. It was........Satan.

"You dunderheads!!!!!!!!!!!!!!!!!!!!!!1111111111" screamed Dumbledore wisely as we went.

I looked around. I wuz in da Slitherin conmen room wiv Satan. I was wearing a blak plaid miniskirt with hot pink fishnetz, a sexy blak MCR corset and blak stiletto boots with pink pentagroms on dem. My earrings were blake Satanist sins and my raven hair was all around me to my mid-black.

"Hey kool where iz dis?" he asked in an emo voice.

"Dis is da future. Dumbeldore's iPod dat he tried to take away from me wuz really also a tim machine." I told him.

"Kool what's an ipatch?" he whimpered.

"It's somefing u use 2 lizzen 2 music." I yakked.

"OMFG kool wait whatz a 4-letter-wurd 4 dirt?" he esked in his sexah voice.

"Um I guezz sand????" I laid confuesdly.

"Yah I wuz just triinyg to make sure u were stil da same perzon." He triumphently giggled.

Suddenly some of my friends walked in.

"OMG you're fucking alive!" said Ginny wearing a blak leather jocket,

blak baggy pants and a goffik black Frum First to Last shirt. I explained 2 her why I was alive.

"Konichiwa, bitch." said Willow. She was wearing a blak corset showing off her boobs with lace all around it and red stipes on it. With it she waz wearing a blak leather miniskirt, big blak boots, white foundation, blak eyeliner, red eyeshadow, and blak lipstick.

"Hey, motherfucker." Said Diabolo with his red hair. He waz wearing a black P?ATD t-shit and blak baggy pants.

"Hey whose that, Ibony?" B'loody Mary questioned as she walked in wearing a black t-shit with a red pentarom on it with lace at the bottom, red letther pants with blak lace, and black stolettoes.

"Oh its Satan." I told her and she nodded knowing da truth.

Suddenly Satan started to cry.

"Are you okay Satan?" we asked concernedly.

"OMFG ur from da future!!1! What if u don't like m anymore koz were from difrent times?????" he asked.

"No I still like you." I said sexily to him.

"Ok." He said ressuredly. I let him lizzen 2 Teenagers by MCR on my ipod while I was about to go outside to find out some fingz. I gave Diabolo a signal to keep Satan occupied. Satan fell asleep. I took the iPod. I was about to walk outside. Profesor Sinister ran in!!!!!!!1111 She was wearing a gothic blak minidress with depressing blak stripes, white and blak stripped tights, and red converse shoes. She was wearing LOTS of blak iliner.

"Oh my fucking god, where's Draco!!!!111 How did Snap get back

here!!! I tohot he wuz in Azerbaijan." I asked sadly.

"Ebony I was so worried abott u but I know you can't fucking die because you're a vrompire. Snape came back because that girl Britney freed him. I never liked her she was a bad student." Trevolry said reassuredly.

"That bitch!!!!!!!11 Did she also free Hargrid and Loopin?" I shouted angrily. I hated Britney because she was a fucking prep.

"Yes they are on the loose at this school. Dumblydore is back Cornelia is on his way to help evry1. Tell evry1 u see to lock themselves in their conman room!!!!!!" Trevolry said worriedly.

"OK. But where's Dracko???? How cum he was doing it with Snap?????"

"I dunno why but I know he almost tried 2 commit suicide after he saw u almost kill urself." she said.

"OMG dat's terrible!!!!!!!!" I gasped. Satan was still asleep, so he couldn't tell what was going on. Then I said "Lizzen evry1, I have sumthing imptent to do. in hr evry1 stay!!!!!!!!!" wiv dat I ran out.

"Good luck Tara!!!!!!!11" everyone cried.

I ran sexily down the staris in2 da Grate Hall while da portraits around looked at me scaredly. There was hardly ne1 else in the stairs nd tere was an atmosphere of horrer. On da way I saw Britney laughing on da stairs. She was wearing a a slutty pink shirt wiv flowers on it, a blu jean skirt Abercromie and pink stiletoos. She looked jest like a pentagram of those fucking preps Hilery Duff and Lindsey Lohan.

"You fucking bitch!!!!!111" I shouted angrily.

"No, your totally a bitch. Now Voldemort will like totally kill u!" she laughed.

"Crucious!!!!!!!!!1" I shouted selectively pontificating my blak wand and she started screaming koz she was being tortured and I laughed sodistically.

"No!!!!!!1 Help me!!!!!!1 Please!!!!!!!!!1" Britney screamed terrifiedly.

I put up my middle finger at her. In her hand I saw da video camera Snape and Lumpin had used to take da video of me. I put the tape of Voldimort doing it with Hedwigg onto it. Then I continued to rown down the stairs with the camera. When I had reached da Grate Hall I saw Vampire Potter. "OMG Vampira!!!!111" I yielded.

We hugged each udder happily. He locked at me wif his gothic red eyes and spiky blak hair. Around them were blak eyeliner and iShadow. His He wus wearing a blak leather Jackson, ledder pants, a Panik at da Disko concert shirt and his blak congress shoes. He looked mor like Joel from Good Charlote than ever. *(did u hear der song da river it rox!!!1)*"I wus so worried you died!" moaned Vampire.

"I know but Im a vampire lol. When I woke up I wuz back in 1980, so neway I bought Voldimort from when he was yung with me."

"Where's Draco?" I asked spuriously.

"Draco? You mean that fukking poser who betroyed you?" Vampir snarkled with anger in his sexy voice.

"I NO BUT WE HAV 2 FIND HIM." I SED SMARTY.

"I'll do it den." Harry said angstily.

"OK." I argreed. Suddenly..........all da lights in da room went out. And den.......da Dork Mark appeared.

"Oh my fucking satan!!!!!" Harry shouted.

"I fink Voldimort has arrivd." I sed anxiously. "Fuck, I have to find Draco!!1 I guess we shood separate."

"Ok." Vampire sed diapperating. Sadly I ran into the Great Hall.

Chapter 43.

AN: I fink after dis I wil hav abott 2 or three mor chapterz. Fangz 2 all muh revyooers not das flamers if u flamed sis story den u suk!!!!!!!!!!111111 if u flam den fukk u!!!111

XXXXXXXXXXXXX666XXXXXXXXXXXXXXXXXX

I walked sexily into the Great Hall. It was empty except for one person. Draco was there!! He sat der in deddly bloom in his blak 666 t-shirt and his baggy blak pants. He had slit his wrists!!!!!111 I felt mad at him for

having sexwith Snape but I felt sorry for him. He looked just like Gerard Way with his red eyes and his pale white face.

"Draco are you okay????" I asked.

"I'm not okay." he screamed depressedly. I thought of the MCR song nd I got even more depressed koz that song always makes me cry. I gave him a pot cigarette and he started to smoke it.

"Oh Draco why did you do it with that fucking bastard Snape?" I asked teardully.

"I-" Draco began to say but suddenly Lupin and Mr. Norris appearated in2 da room!! They didn't see us.

"Im so glad we me and Snape were freed." said Loopin.

"Dam, this job would be great if it wasn't 4 da fukking students!" Mr. Norris argreed.

"Pop addelum!!!!!111" I yielded angrily pointing my wand at them.

"Noooooooo!!!!1" Lupin shouted as chains came on him. Mr. Norris ran away.

"You fukking perv." I said laughing wiv depths of evil and depressedness in my voice. "Now u have 2 tell us where Voldimort is or I'm gong 2 torture u!!!!"

"I don't now where he is!!!!1111" said Loopin. Suddenly Satan and Vampire ran in2 da room. Vampir didn't know who Satan was really.

"Oh my satan, we were so worried about u guys!!1" Vampire said. I looked sexily at Draco with his goffik red eyes with contacts, blak t-shirt that said 666 on it and pale skin like Gerord Way, Vampir with his sexy

blak hair and red eyes just like Frank Iero and Satan who looked jist like Brandan Urie then.

I selectively took the caramel from my pocket. And then..... I began frenching Draco sexily. Loopin gasped. Draco began to take all of his cloves off and I could see his white sex-pack. Then Vampire took his own clotes off too. We all began making out 2gther sexily. I took off my blak leather bra, my blak lace thong and the rest of my clothes. Every1 took their glocks out except 4 me im a girl lol. "Oh mi satan!! Draco!!!!" I screamed as he put his hardness in my thingy Den he did da same fing to Harry. I began making out wiv Satan and he joined in. "OMS!!!111" cried Vampire. "Oh Vampire! Vampire!!!" I screamed screamed. "Oh Satan!!!!!" yelled Harry in pleasore. Loopin watched in shock. Wee took turns doing torture curses on him koz we were all sadists. Suddenly.................................

...........a big blak car that said 666 on the license plate flew strait through da windows. And Snap wuz in it!!!!!!!!11

Chapter 44.

AN: well I hav noffing 2 say but evrt1 stup glamming ok!!111 if any gofik ppl r reading dis den u rok!!!11 omg I stil kant wait 4 da movie!!!1 tom fleton is so hot lol i hop harry wil bekum gofik koz mi frend told me he iz rlly emo in dis book!!!!1111 omfg im leeving dubya pretty soon kant wait!!! Diz wil prolly be da last chaptah until I kum bak.

XXXXXXXXXXXXXX666XXXXXXXXXXXXXXXXXXXXXX

"Dat's mi car!!!!" shooted Draco angrily. But suddenly it was revealied

who was in da car. It wuz…………Snape!!!!!

"I shall free you Loopin but first you must help me kill these idiotic donderheads." he said cruelly from the car as it flew circumamcizing above us. "Ebony Dark'ness Dementia Raven Way must be killed. Den the Dork Lord shall never die!!!!"

"You fucking prep!!!" yelled Draco. Then he loked at me sadly. "I forgot to tell u, Ebony. Snape made me do it with him. I didn't really have sexx him but he's a ropeist!!!!"

We all put our clothes on quickly except Satan. We were so scarred!!!!1 But Satan didn't change. Instead he changed into a man with gren eyes, no nose, a gray robe and white skin. He had changed into…………
Voldemont!!!!!!!111

"I knew who thou were all along." he cackled evilly and sarcastically at me. "Now I shall kill thee all!!!!!!" Thunder came in da room.

"No plz don't kill us!" pleaded Vampire. Suddenly Willow, B'loody Mary, Diabolo, Ginny, Drocula, Fred and Gorge, Hargrid, McGonagall, Dumblydore, Serious and Lucian all ran in.

"What is da meaning of dis?" Dumblydore asked all angrily and Voldimort lookd away *(bcos dumblydore is da only whizard he is scared of.)* He did a spell and suddenly his broomstick came to him sexily. Volxemort flew above the roof evilly on his broomstik.

"Oh my goth!" Slugborn gosped. *(geddit kos im goffik)*

"The Dark Lord shall kill all of you. Then you must submit to him!!!!" Snape ejaculated menacingly.

"You fucking preppy fags!" Serious shouted angrily.

"I know a four-letter word 4 dirt, CRUCIATUS!!!" screamed Harry but da sparks from his wand only hit Draco's car. It fell down Snap quickly crowled out of it and picked up the cideo camera.

"Oh my fucking god!!!1" I cried becoze the video of me in da bathrum, the video of me dong it wif Drako and the video of Satan doing it with

"If you kill me then deze cideos will be shown to everyone in the skull. Then u can be just like that goffik girl Paris Hillton." He laughed meanly.

"No!" I scremed. "FYI I hav da picter of u doing it with Loopin!!!!11"

"Whats she talking abott??????" Lupin slurped as he sat in chains.

"I saw 2 she's gunna show evry1 da picter!!!111" Harry shouted angrily.

"Shut up!!!111'" Lumpkin roared.

"Foolish ignoramuses!!!!!!" yielded Voldemort from his broomstick. "Thou shall all dye soon."

"Think again you fucking muggle poser!!!!!1" Harry yelled and then he and Diablo and Navel both took out blak guns! But Voldimort took out his own one.

"U guyz are in a Latin stand-of!!!!!!!111" I shouted despariedrly.

"Acco Nevel's wand!!!11" cried Voldrimort nd suddenly Nevil's wind was in his hands. "Now I shall kill thee all and Evony u will die!!!!!!!!11111"

He maid lighting come all over da place.

"Save us Ebony!" Dumbledark cried.

I cried sexily I just wanted 2 go 2 the commen room and slit my wrists with mi friends while we watched Shark Attak 3 and Saw 2 and do it with Draco but I knew I had 2 do somefing more impotent.

"ABRA KEDABRA!!!!!!!!!!!11111" I shooted.

THE END

My Immortal 2: Wake Me Up Inside

Yep, the Sekwel that wasnt really a sekwel. Enjoy while you can. i might delete it completely, unless the admins get to it first. Flame me if you want, I dont give a fuck.

Chapter 1.

AN: Srry dat I havnt riten any nu chaps, but sum1 hakd my old akont, & nw I hav 2 use dis 1. If yu dnt lik goffik stuff thn yu a prepz, so fuk of!!11

XXXXXXXXXXX666XXXXXXXXXXXX

I lookd at Voldrimort as he flw bck, httn da wall.

"Yu wll pay 4 dis", he sad sexily.

I tied 2 close my eys nd fink abot Pete Wentz and his sexynis. I cudnt bar da pain anymore. Al I wnatd wuz 2 g 2 my rom and cut my rists.

"Yu r al lik da rst", I said suacialy. "Al yu wnt 2 du is lrd it ovr us goffz. Yu dicktate wat we cn nd cnt du, yu mtherfukr".

"Hw dar yu tlk 2 me lik dat", Woldermort sid as he buort out his wip, nd bgan 2 wip me. I cried sexily. I thried to fink abot Pet Wentz nd hs sexy boby, bt da foght kep goin awy.

"Sum1 help me", I cried saucialy.

Sudenly cam Samaro, Vampires dad.

"Di", He siad as he gut hiz gun ut and shot Voldsermort.

"ARRRRRRRRRR" Voldadork yeld as he flw awy on his broom. I trid 2 find Samaro but he wuz gone!!111

XXXXXXXXXXXXXXXXXXXXXXXXXXXXXXXXXXXXX

AN: Wuz dat good. If yu flme it, dan yu a prep!!1

Chapter 2.

AN: Dis is da nects chptr. Dnt flame yu posers!!1111

XXXXXXX666XXXXXXXXXX

Dombledor went up 2 a prap named Britney and sid, "Well done Britney, you hav savd us once agin"

WHAT DA FUK", I yelded at him. "I Did al tghart hard wrk, yu mthrfukr".

"Ebony Dark'ness Dementia Raven Way, yu did noffing as we wre bing turtured by da Dirk lord. Yu wll be snt to yu room".

Dat nite I creid. That bitch took all da cridit. Tht mthrfukr will pay!!

XXXXXXXXXXXXXXXXXXXXXXX

Da mext day, a new grl strtd at skool. C wuz anther fukn prep. Her name will Paris Hilton. C hd only fond out dat c wuz a qwitch nt dat long ago and c mde sure to b mean to us goffs.

C spilld aflass of wtar on Vampire.

"Y da fuk did yu do that, yu bitch", I yeld dat hr.

"Watch da mouuth", c said.

Aftr c wuz gne, I lokd at Draco, noing dat he wanted 2 do it wtih me.

XXXXXXXXXXXXXXXXXXXXXXXXX

AN: Dont fukn flame, yu psers.

Chapter 3.

Dnt fukn flam me yu bitchs. I bt yu a prep!!1111 Dis capt is 4 Raven, yu wll alwys be in our haerts.

XXXXXXXXXXX666XXXXXXXXXXXX

Dat nite, me and Draco went to our rooms. Draco tok hus top off, and I did da smae.

He began to sux on my boobs. I sexily cried out in pian. His mouth tasted tendr. He den stoped, and look at me. He lokd lik Gerald Way. He den went and tok is paints off. I saw his you know wat, and began to sux on it. Draco creied sucidally as I suxed on it.

"Stop it" he yelled sexly.

While I stll had his you know what in his mouth, I siad, "if you wus out know, yu r prep".

"Don't fuken tell me wat to do, Draco yelled at me sexily. He then lieftd the room nakd.

I cudnt bare it. So I cut my slf wile listn to the radio.

"Another turning point a fork stuck in the road Time grabs you by the wrist directs you where to go So make the best of this test and don't ask why It's not a question but a lesson learned in time It's something unpredictable but in the end it's right I hope you had the time of your life" da band sang.

"Evn da radio is mocking me now", I fukn yelld.

XXXXXXXXXXXXXXXXXXXXXXXXXXXXXXXXXXXXXX

AN: I hope dat wuz good. Pleaz no flamez!!111

Chapter 4.

AN: Don't kukn flame me yu prepz. Yu only jeluz!!111 Catn wayt 4 da new FOB albun!! Pete Wntz loks so hot!!1

XXXXXXX666XXXXXXXXX

Da next day, my bnd strtd 2 ply. Craco dcided 2 qit da bnd cuz of wat we did lst nite. I wuz wrin a blck GC top whch wuz ripd and shrt lethr skrt, whch wuz also ripd. I hd blck liptick on nd wite fondason and blck eylinr. I had a pntagrm ncklce around my nck and I had a ponty hi-heeld bots. My har wuz al mesd up. I wor blck ey contcts. We dcided to rite sum nu songz. 1 of dem wuz cald "Brak 3 of da system". We plyd it and evry1 luvd it.

"To da depf of hell. Wher Satan ringz hiz Belz Goffs of da worldz Slit da rist 2 da beat" I sang.

We den plyed sum oldr songz. Theal luvd it.

"We die 4 noffing Bledn our rist our Let our lifs be none 4 our pact b cmpete", I sang da next songz.

Bitney and da nu grl cam up and sad dat we wer lam. Ill shw dat bitch!!111 C puld da plg, wat a bitch!!1

We wre tld to lave cuz da tcherz tld us 2. Fuk them. Dey alwd prepz msc 2 b plyd lik dat fukn bitch Paris hu sonded lik SHIT!!111111

"Y cnt dey ply stuf lik My Chem *(If u don't no dey r den fuk off!!)* cuz dat is rel musc", I fukn yeld at them sexily!!.

"Dat is is a detntion Elbony", said da tcher. FUKN BITYCH!!

Chapter 5.

AN: Y da fuk r yu al sayn im nt me? Wlll I am!!1111 So fuk of yu preps!!111

XXXXXX666XXXXXXXXX

Me and Bloody Mary were sitn outsid wen we saw a postr cum up. It sed dat FOB were playn dat nite.

"I so luv FOB", sad Vloody Mary.

"Yea, but I cnt stand Pete anymor, snce he gos out wth dat bitch Ashlee (Why cunt c fukn die!!1111). But I stll luv der nu song", I rplid.

So dat nite we got chnged in2 sum nu clth dat I gt frm Hot Topc *(if u dont no wat dat is, den fuk off)*. Wat I wor wuz a blck korset wit wuz ripd and a

blud red leather miniskrt. I had blud lipstik on aswll. I had lng blck lethr army bots aswel whch were tite as.

When we gt dar we saw sum of our frendz nd we wtched FOB playd. Dey wre amzng. Pete Wentz lukd as evr.

Patrick sng dar bst I evr herd.

"I don't blame you for being you But you can't blame me for hating it So say, what are you waiting for? Kiss her, kiss her I set my clocks early 'cause I know I'm always late" Patrick sang.

It wuz so amzng dat I had a orge.

Aftr da shw, me nd Bloddy Mary brorte FOB cncrt tees nd gt Pete nd Patrik 2 sgnd dem.

"Dat wuz so fukn kol siad Blodoy Nary.

XXXXXXXXXXXXXXXXXXXXX

AN: If yu dunt thnk dat im rely me den fuk off.

Chapter 6.

AN: Y da fuk r u al bng meen 2 me. U gt noider wat its ik bng goff, u fukn prepz!!1 Jst fuk off!!111 Y cnt u tak me sireusly? Im a jok 2 u r u. den fuk off!! Raven, I so fukn mis u, y didu hav2 hng urslf.

XXXXXXXX666XXXXXXXX

Me & Bloody Mayr wnt in2 da tolet gt out of our we bgan psh agnst ech othr. I flt hr swet on my skn.

"Hu neds guys wen we hv ech othr, c told me.

"I fukn hat Droco", I ylded sixily, "I bt he is chetn onme by hvng it wif Vampire. Hes dne it bfor".

We den sat dwn nd listnd 2 sum GC whle sltn our rist. Den aftr dat, we den wnt bck 2 our roms. On our way, we sw Draco wth dat slut, Paris. He wuz wearn prepz clthin.

"U BASTED!!11" I yled sucacidally. "FUK OFF".

He den wnt 2 da boys tolets, mst likly 2 hav sexs.

Wile we wlkd bck 2 our roms, we gt anothr detenton frm Mr Noris. Dat basted mst fukn di fr wat he put me thru!!11.

XXXXXXXXXXXXXXXXXXx

AN: Im a goff, cuz u dnt no wat u r tlkin abut.

Chapter 7.

AN: Stp flming me, u prepz!!11 Fuk u als Justin, u tretd me lik sht 4 lung!!1 Thnk 2 my sis 4 da spnsh stff

XXXXXXXX666XXXXXXXX

Da nxt day, I wok up frm my coffn, whch hd blud red covern, iv chnged it cuz I gt bred of my old 1. I gt changd into a blck shrt skrt wth red stps, nd da GC top I gut frm da cncert I wnt 2. I putt on a blc tigt lethr jckit, and sum lng biits dat wnt up 2 my nees. My har wuz al mst up, nd I hd blck mke up on. I hd blud red ey cntacks on.

we hd a nu techr. He wuz relly hot nd he spke rely god spnish. Je lokd

alut lik Joel frm GC!!

"Hopla nnos, cmo eta ustd esa nchi. Mi nombre es vandersleld paro ustd pude todo lamida yo Sombra. Apremderemos hay sbre pesidilas", he tld us. He spke so sexy dat I almst hd a orgnisb. We begn 2 wrk. He wuz der 2 rplace dat pervat Lupun.

"Heso hot", sad Blody Matry.

"Iso wun2 go out wif him, I sadi. I ddnt cuz Draco hd jsut chetd on me wif dat slut Bitney.

So we wnt awy 2 our rum 2 slt our ristz, wile lisnin to da Ing Lif & def by GC *(if yu dunt no wat sng dat is, den fuk off!!1)*.

XXXXXXXXXXXXXXXXXXX

AN: Dunt fukn flam me!!1 Da reson y my wrtn nt god at dat momnt is dat my profredr is died. I cunt do anifing abut dan!! Raven, Ido dis 4 u. RIP 1992-2008

Chapter 8: The Jetset Life Is Gonna Kill You

AN: Dnt fukn flame me u prepz!!11 Dis is 4 u Raven RIP 1992-2008.

XXXXXX616XXXXXXX

Da nxt clas, dmbldor calld me up 2 his ofice. He wuz dis tiem wering a MCR top (dat fukn poser).

"Dis is vry importnt stuf Enoby", he tlled me. "Smap nd Lupim hs escabe. Day wll b tukn 4 u. U r in fanger".

"Dey bettr nt tri n tak pics of me nakd agan. I dunt wnted 2 be lik da slut

pasis. I dunt wnt aex taps of me on da net", I ylled foffikly.

"Cam dwn, Ebobyu. Al u hve 2 do is kep a klow cober, cuz snaop and lupn can b lukn anywer", dubldork said 2 me sucidaly.

"Gret", I yled sixely, "I nw hav pervrts aftr me, grest".

I ran bak 2 da commnrum nd slopd my rst wil listning 2 Hold On by GC. Al I wnted 2 do wuz kil myslf. I deicded 2 bed. But wen I gt my rum, I saw Smape der. Bloody Mayr wuz der bt c wuz dead. I sw al thes bum wunds on her bdy.

"Di u mothrfukr", I yled at snpe.

XXXXXXXXXXXXXXXX

AN: Don't fukn rport me us posers!!11

Chapter 9: Chapter 10.

AN: Y dnt u bliev dat it is relly me? Is it cuz dar so mny poser hu fink dat dey can btend 2 b me? Cuz Im da reel Tara.

XXXXXX666XXXXXXX

Sexly, Sombre cam in nd jickd Smap ut of da windo. Snap yled sucidally as he fel 2 da flor.

"Cum wif me, Sombre tld me saxily.

So I folo hm 2 Dumblidarks ofist. Wen I gt der, I sw Dunblidorf penixs. It

wuz red nd hot.

Dumblidor wnt up 2 me. He wuz woryd.

"I is nt saf 4 u 2 b hre. Infct it is nt saf 4 any1 2 b here now. Dis skool must b lose dwn", he tld every1 in da offise.

Pro Gondagol smild. Dat bitch wnted dis skool dwn 4 ages. Fugde lukd hppy. He did nt hav 2 deel wif da skol anymor, so dat wuz gud 4 him. Hanrid wuz sad. He luvd dis skool so mch.

All I wnted 2 do wuz go 2 my room nd slit my rist. I cudnt bar it. I nu I hd 2 go home...

Chapter 10: I am a big FAT troll

Authors Note: This is not Tara. I have hacked into her account, and I will rather keep my name secret, fearing that a crazy goff/emo kid might murder me. Enjoy.

.ooooooooo911oooooooo.

Suddenly Dumbledore decided to get rid of the evil Enoby once and for all.

"Let us cut our wrist", he told everyone in the office. "Here is a knife that I have convenently have on me".

Enoby could not wait to cut herself. So she quickly ran up to Dumbledore and grapped the knife out of his hand. Like in an epic scene in a movie, in which in all the trailers have in them, Enoby cut her wrist. Suddenly, she dropped dead.

Everyone begins to sing, "Yay, the Goff is dead".

.oooooooooooooooooooo.

So after this event, it was discovered the all the sex scenes in the first story was all in Enobys head, and that the sex in Chapter 3 was Enoby

forcing Draco to have sex.

Snape and Lupin were not sex addicts, but trying to prove that Enoby was illegally cutting herself and being Goff, which was illegal within the wizardry community, for it was to muggle like. This was however was proven when Enoby cut herself, and died.

Bloody Gothic Rose 666 renamed themselves I Love My Life, and they began to sing Preppy songs instead of Goffic songs, which wasn't a real genre in the first place.

Good Charlotte, My Chemical Romance and Fall Out Boy never played at Hogwarts, but instead was in Enobys head, which all her so called friends played along to keep her happy. They were afraid that she would killed herself if she found out.

And to end this story, lets have a Britney Spears song be played over the credits:

Oh baby baby How was I supposed to know that somethin' wasn't right here oh baby baby I shouldn't have let you go And now you're out of sight, yeah Show me how you want it to be tell me baby 'cause I need to know now oh, because My loneliness Is killing me (and I) I must confess I still believe (still believe) When I'm not with you I lose my mind give me a sign hit me baby one more time

.oooooooooooooooooooo.

Disclamer: I do not own any of this stuff, not even Enoby (pulls a sad faces).

'

Chapter 11.

AN: Hu da fuk hakd my acont? Its nt fnny!!1

XXXXX6666XXXXX

I cudnt believ it. I wuz stndng at da trian as I waitd 2 gt on. Vampire wuz der, wif a dreprezzd luk on his fac.

"Wat is r0ng?" I askd hm.

"My unc nd unt hat goffik peps. Ill hav 2 gt chnge b4 I gt hme", Vampire tld me.

I bgan 2 cri secily. I cudnt bar hving nt 2 b goffik 4 dat lng tme. I flt so srry 4 Vampire dat I wnted 2 slit my rist.

I wll e u 2 ceek up on u", I sad 2 hm. All he did wuz fround.

"dunt tll dem dat im hu I am", he tld her.

Da trantip wuznt dat lng. We rote sum nu Bloody Gothic Rose 666 sngs, whch were gud.

Den I gt 2 da staton nd der watng wuz my lit bro Milo Agenesis Way...

XXXXXXXXXXXXXXX

AN: Ive gt a nu bf Gareth Vandersleld nd I fink I wll b abl 2 do it wif hm. Dunt flam me u prepz!!11

Chaptr 12.

AN: Dnt flme me u rpeps!!11 Its nly cuz ya jeluz!!111 Gareth u r my onli reson 4 dis gud 4 nofink lif

XXXXX666XXXXX

I wnt 2 my rum. It wuz all drk, cuz I hatd da lite. 2 da sde, der wuz my

cofn, whch wuz covr wif prple slk. Al ovr da walls wuz postrs of GC, MCR, FOB, P!daDisko, nd Evrnescent. In my cubid wuz my goffik clths dat I gt frm Hot Topik.

I gt chnged in2 a shrt skrt dat wuz ripd, a MCR *(der goifk)* top, nd a lethr jakt. I hd all my ovr my face, lik a emo *(Cuz Emo nd Gokik IS DA SAME THINH!!1)* os dat no1 cud se my ugly fac. I wor blk liptik, whte pwdr ovr my face, nd blck ilinr. I hd a peer of blck chuks on.

My lit bro Milo wuz werng a GD *(C der r gokik too)* top, wif tigh jens on. His hiar wuz al spickd up. His skn wuz pale, nd his teef wer drwling 4 blud. His chcks were blud red, nd he hd a hatrd luk on his fase.

I wnt 2 da diner tble nd nd we hd human meet, all covrd in blud, cuz al my famli is vampirs, nd r aalso gofik. Der wuz no lite on cuz we hatd da lite. I dnk diet coke mixd wif blood, cuz Im a vapire.

Aftr dat, we wtchd on tv a persn hav his blud suxd by a vampir. We den slit our rists whle listn 2 GD. Den my mun nd dad wnt 2 der rum. Me nd my lit bro Mili wtchd da nitemare b4 xmas, nd den corsb brde, nd we tok herion, nd slit our rist again.

I decded 2 chek up on my flks. I wnt 2 my rum, nd luk insid nd I saw my mon nd Hugrid nakd on da bed doin it. I sucidaly has a orgnism.

"Wat da fuk", I yeld at her, "Wat da fuk r u doin".

My dad wlkd in, shck, cuz had jst done it wif b4 hnd.

"Y", he yled sixely. "Y did u hav 2 do dis 2 me".

He wlkd off & so did i. I wlk awy, so da prk, wer I slit my rist. All I wntd 2 do wuz kil mislf. Y did dey hav 2 do dat. Suddnly, I saw a postr get put up, whch said dat Panik da Disko wer playng in my twon. I cudnt beliebv it.

XXXXXXXXxXXXX

AN: Dunt fukn flme me u prps. U r only jeluz!!111111 Gofik is a wrd!!1 nd im nt a wanabe, I AM A GOFF!!1111 Do u evn no wat a gof rely is!! Dat cuz u a prep!!111 So Fuk oF!!

Chapter 13.

AN: Dunt fukn flam me u prepz!!11 my ritng nd spllng is alrite!!1111

XxXxXxXxX666XxXxXxXxX (C ive chnged dat, r u k wif dat, or do u stll hat me)

Dat day, I wnt & gt tikets. Da day of da concrt, I invted Vampier. His unc nd ant fought he wuz gng 2 a rep shw, so dey ddnt mnd. He pikd me up in hs blck merc, whch had blud red lethr sheets. He wuz werng a Panik! top, nd tite blck jens, whch were ripd. Hs hair wuz nt blck, lik he usely hd, bt munly blu. I kisd him nd I hd an orgnism.

In da car, we smked pot, nd gt al hi. I red a drepresing bok, nd we listnd 2 MCR, and den we listnd 2 P!daDisko. We den slt our rits, whle listning to GC. We den gt 2 da concrt.

We gt 2 da frnt of da crwd nd mshed rite out frnt. I saw Urie, nd I hd a orgnism.

"Dey r so fukn kool!?" I yled.

"Yeh, bt dey r nt as kool as u r", Vapire said to me saxily. He kisd me agan nd I hd an anther oranism.

"Time is never time at all you can never ever leave without leaving a piece of youth and our lives are forever changed we will never be the same the more you change the less you feel believe, believe in me, believe", da bnd sung.

"I so luv dis sng. Ths has 2 b der bst one deyve ritn", I tld vampire sucidaly.

"Sam, bt I luv u bettr!!", he sexily.

I wnt awy 2 by sum Panik! tops, bt on my way, I sw a goffik kid dat I sen b4:

It wuz Satan........

Chapter 14.

AN: Dunt fukn flam me u rpz!!1

XXXXXX666XXXXXX

"Di", I yled hm as I puuld a smll.

"Stp he sed" Im nt Woldanort. I wuz kdnapd b4 da Marylin Mansn shw".,

so is wuznt u al da tim", I sed 2 hm

"Yah, & I ned 2 tll u sumfing", He sed 2 me. "U hav 2 fnd da bll ofda furchar. It wll tech u hu 2 dfet Voldimort".

Wer is is it"? I askd hm.

"In da Minisy", He tld me. "dat hll nct 2 da on dat Vampires Gdfafa gts klld".

As he sed dat, he wuz movd awy by da crwd. I dcid 2 by da tps, nd wnt bak 2 Vampire.

"We gt 2 go fnd dos bllz" I sed 2 hm

"okuy"m, he sed.

XXXXXXXXXXX

AN: im nt a jok, im bng seryus!!111111 dunt flme u rpapz!!111

Chapter 15: I Write Sins Not Tragedies

AN: Dat is a P!daDisko sng, I herd dem ply it liv!!11 U dunt no anyfng prep!!1 Dis chap hs a bg twst 2 da stry!? RIP Raven 192-2008 I Luv U

XXXXXX555XXXXXXX

We dcided 2 mos abt mor. So we moshd rite da frnt, lukng in2 Urie secily Is. He wuz so ht dat I gt an orgy.

"When the lights are dim and your heart is racing as your fingers touch his skin. I've got more wit, a better kiss, a hotter touch, a better fuck Than any boy you'll ever meet, sweetie you had me Girl I was it, look past the sweat, a better love deserving of Exchanging body heat in the passenger seat? No, no, no, you know it will always just be me", Urie sng. Dey ddnt ply ani of der nu stuuf cuz dat stuuf wuz prep musc!!1111 & if suxd.

Afta dey wnt of stge, we watd 4 da bakup bnd 2 cum on. We dcded 2 tolet & we didit. Vapire pt hs stik fingy in2 my u no wat, & da likwed stuuf bgan 2 enta mi u no wat. I screemd suciadaly as he redrew da stik fingy frm my u no wat. He den wnt & suxd on my b00bz, saxng da mlk frm it. I scremd evn mor.

Afta dat, we slt our rists whle listning 2 da blak perde. We den enjtd heryon in2 our bodys & strted 2 cri in pan.

Afta dat, we wnt out of da tolet 2 listn 2 da bakup bnd. Dey wer waring msk on. Dey wer snging prep musc, lik dat stupd bittney speers sng. Dey toke der msk of.

Dey wer Valfamort & his def esters.............

XXXXXXXXXXX

AN: If u kep flamng me, I wll kil mislef!!1111

Chapter 16 XXXeditdXXX

AN: I dunt car wat u suy, im gong 2 kep ritng diz stry!!111 U cnt kep rportng me, bt i wll kep gong!! dis chpta is scry bdw.

XXXXXXXX666XXXXXXxx

"U shal cnvert or DI!!1111" Voldsmort yeld in dat old qway. Da Def Delas wnt & kild a fw of dat goffx, cuz da ddnt wnt 2 bcum prepz. 1 of dem hd der heed ct of.

"Dat is wat gong 2 hppnd if u dunt cnvrt" he yelf

Der is nowy dat im gong 2 bcum a prep", gof kid yeld. It wuz Coln Grevy, but dat wuz nt wat dey cld hm animore. He wuz nw cald Reapa. He dscovd dat hs rul fafer wuz a mss kila. So he bcam goff & jond Slivalin.

"Tho nt dar spek 2 me lik dat", Voldaermort yeld sucidaly.

"We wll bw 2 u"m, he yled.

Voldabort id a spll dat cud hav klld hm, bt I jmbd & gt hm outof da wey. We kwickly gt awy. I cudnt gt ova wat hd hapn. Me, Repa & Vampir wnt bak 2 da tolet 2 slt our rist cuz of wat hd happnd. I wnted hm 2 di!!111 We dcided nt 2 g bak der. I hopd P!dadisko wer saf cuz der wud b kild if Voldernor fond out dat dey wer goff.

XXXXXXXXXXXXXXXXX

AN: I hop diz wuz bata? 2 dos hu dnt lik da rap bit, i gt rid of it. Nw r u fin??

Chapter 17.

AN: Dis is da nu chap. Iv gt a nu beta cld shadwkng. So der is no reson 2 flam me animor!!111111

XXXXXXX666XXXXXX

We quickly got through the people who had become preps because of what Voldemort had done. We walked down the road as quickly as we could. We tried to find Vampire's car, which was parked nearby.

When we got there, it had been destroyed!

"Oh My God!" I yelled sadly, "What are we gonna do?!"

"It looks like we are gonna have to walk home," Reapa said.

"But that's miles away, how can we do that?" I asked him.

I looked around & there was a demon. It was wearing black cloaks, & it floated in the sky. It was a dementor. We began to run cause we knew that they sucked the life out of you. But we were too late. It was beginning to suck on Reapa.

"No!" I yelled, as the dementor was sucking the life out of Reapa. "Do something, Vampire!"

Vamire got out his wand & summoned a stag patronus that killed the dementor. We were safe again.

But Reapa wasn't. He was dying. The sight of him dying made me want to slit my wrist, but I didn't have the time, as the Death Eaters were coming.

XXXXXXXXXXXXXXXXXXX

AN: I hop dat wuz betta? No flamng plez!!1111

Chapter 18.

Here is the edited version of the next chapter...

By the time we got back to the house, it was burnt down. It was a big shock cause no one expected it at all.

"So what are we going to do now," Vampire asked Tara. "Where will we go to now?"

"I bet it's the Death Eaters that did this to me. They know where I live. OMG, where are all my clothes?!" I screamed suicidally. Vampire tried to calm me down, but it was no good. I wanted to kill myself.

"We will get back at them, those preps, those bastards!" Vampire said to me. He was as angry as I was. What were we to do. I had nowhere to go at all. I was homeless.

Because of this, me and Vampire slit our wrists while listening to MCR's "I don't love you". I cried because I lost my clothes. Those fucking BASTARDS! They will fuckin' pay!

I decided to call a friend. I called her up, and she said, "What is it, my bitch!"

"I've got a prob," I told her, "my house is burnt down! Please pick me up!"

So as we were waiting, Vampire took his pants off, and I took mine off too! He then jizzed in my mouth. Then, after that, he put his throbbing manhood into my muff, and we did it. I then grabbed his balls and he screamed sexily as I did that. But it wasn't the same as Draco, with his lips, and how he looked like Joel from GC. He was so fucking hot. Hot in his jeans, why did he dump me, that fucking bastard, he must fucking die! I couldn't keep doing it, cause I kept thinking of Draco and his sexy eyes!

It was then that Willow, my friend, pulled up in a van. She looked so hot with what she wore. With the shirt, black mini skirt with red stripes, and her messy hair, she was fuckin' hot! She was wearing pink crocs and tight black jeans!

"Come in," she said.......

XD is needing editing fangz!

Chapter 19.

AN: Diz is da nxt chapd, fnagz 2 Shado 4 luking thru diz stuff, u fukn rox!!1111
Flame diz den u r rep!!111

XXXXXXXXXXX666XXXXXXXXXXXXXXX

Newest chapter: edited and good to go!...

On the way to Willow's house, we slit our wrists while listening to Teen Spirit by Nirvana (if you don't know them then fuck off you preps!). We then talked about depressing things that made me want to slit my wrists again. I then read a depressing book, which also made me want to slit my wrists. Why the fuck did I keep having these thoughts? Was it cause of me doing it with Vampire? Fuck, I wanted to kill myself.

We then got to her house, which was all goffik and stuff. It looked like an old castle, which had gargoyles all around it. It looked a lot like that house from Edward Scissorhands (if you don't know what that movie is, then FUCK OFF!) We went into the house, and there was all these posters of GC, Panic! At the Disco, Ritex of speing, MCR, FOB, GD, Nirvana, Evanescence, and the other goffik bands. Willow was so fuckin' cool. She was a fuckin' hottie! Man, I wanted to do it with her.

"So, what is wrong?" she said.

"Voldemort has burned my house down, and burnt all my clothes (he must fuckin' pay for what he has done). Stan has told me to look for some ball that is meant to see the future."

"I see," Willow said. She spoke so sexily that I got an orgasm. "This ball can tell us how to defeat the Dark Lord! It will tell us his weakness."

"Cool, then we must look for it now," I said to her.

"No, Emoby, you must stay here and rest, for tomorrow we will look!" she told me.

So we got some food, which was a cow, and some good cat food. It was also covered with blood, and we had blood mixed with milk as well. Before we ate, we prayed to the Devil by humming this:

"*Stan wonderful, Curse this dinner, As youo others. Let them be tortured, Beaten upon, For not accepting you Be the one that will punish them And send them to Hell!*" we hummed. The Devil was pleased.

Den Vampire sed a peom 2 plez da Devil:

I wait all my life to fade into darkness Beneath my bed I keep my rope Which will hang on the day of reckoning Showing the flag of what my life means

They hurt me no more, never again They will me sided with me, not against They will feel the hurt, with the power of guilt They will feel sorry for me at last

It has been sixteen fucking years Since I had to not live with suffering Dead I will be at last, no feelings what so ever I lie there cold and naked, waiting

She left me there to lie in wast She will be one of them to feel the guilt She will end her life, just as I will She will be forgotten, just like me

They were the ones to fuck things up To put me in the shit I am in My one last wish is to see them suffer Like I have suffered for sixteen years

I know that when I'm gone, I will be forgotten I know that when I take the last leap That all will be gone, but that is good From that day on, I will suffer no more

They will find me naked and cold I will talk to them nor move No breath will come from my mouth And then the waiting game will be over

(Fangz 2 Gareth Vandersleld 4 alowing me 2 us diz peom. U rox!!11 666)

After we had finished our food, we slit our wrists, and praised the Devil. We then watched Corpse Bride, which made me want to do it with Vampire. So me and Campfire went to Willow's can and banged around in it. So I sucked onto Vampire's cock and sucked in his creamy load, after which he had an ejaculation and the sperm came out, which I

sucked in as well. Then we began to kiss each other hard. Then my little bro, Milo, came into the van and banged around with us as well. Milo and Vampire sucked on each of my boobs at the same time. Then Milo put his dick into my holy hole. Then Vampire put his penis into Milo's ass, which we watched for an hour, but Milo could not take it anymore, and had to stop it to get out of the car.

"What is wrong?" I asked him. "Don't get all preppy on me!"

"But it's my first time, and I could not take it anymore. I'm only 12." Because I had had enough, and so had Vampire, we went back indoors. Willow got a cat that she had and slit its snout, and gave it up as an offering to Stan.

"Give us better tomorrow and allow us to defeat the preps," she said. She was so fuckin' hot then that I got an orgasm.

XXXXXXXXXXXX666XXXXXXXXXXXX

AN: Hopdat wuz gud? 666 ROX!!1

Chapter 20.

AN: Dis is wat da lst few chaps ment 2 b lik. Dunt funk rport me!!1111

XXXXXXXXXXXX666XXXXXXXXXXXX

Bi da tim we gt bak 2 da hose, it wuz brnt dwn. It wuz a bg shok cuz no1 xpctd it al.

"So swat our we gong 2 du nw", Vamire tlkd tara. "We wll we go 2 nw?"

"I bt itz da def buildas dat sis diz 2 me. Day no wer I livd. OMG, wer r al mi cholthes", I scremd suciali. Vampir trid 2 cam me dwn, bt it wuz no gud. I wntd 2 kil mislef.

"We wll gt bak dem, dos prpz, dos bastd!!" Vampre sed 2 me. He wuz as angi as I wuz. Wat wer we 2 du.i hd noher 2 go al. I wwuz humless.

Cuz of diz, me nd Vampire slt our list wile lixtn 2 MCR I dnt luv u lik I lvu u yestaday!! I creid dta I lst my clthz. Dos fukn BASTD. Dey wll fukn paY!!11111

I dcided 2 rung a friedn. I ringd her up, & c sed, "Wat is it, mi bitchz!!"

"Iv gt a probz", I tlkd her", mi hose is brnut gown!!11, plez pike me up!?"

So az we wer wiatng, Vamire tuk hiz painteez of, & I tuk my of to!!11, He den pizzd in my moth. Dem afta dat, e put hiz shichi thngy in 2 mi u-no-wat, & we did it. I den grapd hiz balz & he scremd saxily as I did dat. Bt it wuznt da sam az Draco, & his lipz, & hw he lukd lik joul frm GC. He wuz so fukn ht. Ht in hiz jens, whi did he dmb me, dat fuknn Bastd, he mst fukin Die!!111. I cudnt kep dong it, cuz I keep finking of Fraco, & hiz secy Iz!!111

It wuz den dat Willow, mi firend puld up in a serena van. She lukd so hot wif wat she wor. Wif da shrt blck mini scrit, wif red strpz, to sa mezzy haor, c wuz fukn hot!!111 C wuz wering pnk chukz, & blck tght jenz!!1

XXXXXXXXXXXXXXXXXXXXXXXXXXXXXXXXXXXXxxx

Cum in", c sed.......

Wil in willowz haice, we slt our ritz wil lztne 2 Teen spirt, by Nirvana (if u dunt no dem den fuk of u prepz!!11). We den tlkd obut deprzzing fingz, dat mad me wnt 2 lit my tits agan. I den red a dprezing buk, wik alzo wntd 2 mak me slt my wist. I da kuk kept havng diz fougt? Wuz it cuz of me dong it wif Vanpire. Fuk I wntd 2 kil mielfd.

We den gt 2 her hoze, whch wuz al goffik & stuuf. It lukd lik an old casstle, whchhad gargilz al arund it. It luk alt lik dat hoze frm Edwrt szizorz handz (if u dunt wat dat move iz, den FUK OFFF!!1111) we wnt in2 da hoze, & der wuz al diz psterz of GC, P!daDisko, Ritex pf speing, MCR, FOB, GD, Nirvsna, Eveneczent, & da otha foffik ndz. Willo wuz so fukn kool. & zhe wuz a fukn hottee!!1111 Man I wntd 2 do it wif hr.

Zo wat iz wrng, "zhe sed.

"Voldamort haz burnd mi houze dwn, & brnt al my cloth (he muzt fukn pay 4 wat he haz don). Stan haz tld me 2 luk 4 sum bll, dat ment 2 c da futor"

"I c", willo ded. C spok so zexily dat I gt an organizm. "Diz bll cn tel uz hw 2 defet da fark lord!!111 it wil tel uz hiz weknizz.

"Kool, den we muzt luk 4 it nw", I sed 2 hr

"No emoby", u muzt sty her & rezt 4 2moro we wil luk!!11111", she askd me.

So we gt sum food, whit wuz a kow, & sum gog kat food. It wuz alzo covrd wif blud, & we hd blud mixd wif mlk az well. B4 we eta, we payd 2 da Devil by hyming diz:

"Stan wndrful Curze diz dina Az u do 2 othas Lt dem b tortad Beetn uon 4 nt akkeptng u b da 1 dat wil punizh dem & snd dem 2 jell!!1111", we humd. Da dvul wuz plezd.

Afta we hd finshd our fud, we slt our riztz, 7 prazd da Devl. We den wtchd da corsb brid, we mad me wnt 2 do it wif Vanire. So me & Campire wnt 2 willoz can & bngd arond in it. So I suxd on2 Vampir u-no-wat & suxd in al hiz pizz, denhe hd an ejecton& da smerm cam ut, whit I suxd in as wel. Den we bgan 2 kiz ech otha hard. Den my lit bro milo cm into da van & bng arong wif uz qell. Nilo & bampire suxd on ech of mi b00bz da samtim. Den milo put hiz u-no wat in2 mi holey fing. Den Vampire put hiz u-no-wat in2 miloz holey fingy, whch we pashd 4 a huor, bot milo cud nt tak it animor, & hd 2 stp it 2 get out or da car.

"Wat iz rong", I azkd him. "unt be a prep onme".

"Bt itz my fixt tim, & I cud nt tak it anomore. Im onli 12". Cuz I hd enogh, & so has Vampire, we wnt bak in doorz. Willlo gt a kat dat c hd & slit itz fout, & gav it up az an offaing 2 stan

"Giv uz betternss 2morro

& alow uz 2 defet dem orep", c sed. C wuz so kukn hot den dat I gt a organizm.

XXXXXXXXXXXXXXXXXXXXXXXXx

AN: I do nt wnt a beta animor as i do nut trst any1 hlping me out wif mi stori otha dan Raven R.I.P

Chapter 21.

AN: Justn, fukn lev mi akont alon!!!!!!!!!11 if u kept hakng in2 dis akont, I fukn rng da polise!!!!!!!!!!1 dis not jok!!!!!!!!!!111 Fnagz agin 4 gereth 4 getng mi akont bak, u fukn fox!!!!!!!!!!!!!!1

XXXXX666XXXXXXXX

So ew gt in2 willow`z sprtpak van, & we derived 2 da minster of majick. We gt ut of da can & wnt 2 da polis box, dat we gt in2, & we wnt in2 da man rum 4 da plac. Der wuz Wurmtail, gardng da Vampir, willow & Milo snekd pas da def deeler, I surduced him.

"Fany abita acton", I aksd hm. He sed yez & he den pt hiz stiky fingy in2 mi u no wat &we di it.

"Sop!!!!!!!!11", I cremd sucialily, cuz I wuz in so muck pan. So I sopd & run of, catng up wif Bampire 7 da otha gis. We wlkd pasd da plase wer Vampire`s dogfafer ded. Vampir cryd vut I camd im dwn. We den gt 2 da plase wer al da orbz wer kept, & we camd acrzz da 1 dat sed Eboby Dementa Dark`ness Raven Way. I pikd it u[, bt sum def buildas wlkd in2 da rum. 1 of dem tuk of der massk.

It wuz............. Draco!!!!!!!!!11111

XXXXXXXXXXXXx

AN: Dat I nt updatd 4 a lng tim, bt da hakd gt diz akont!!!!!1 So fangz 4 da suprt. 2 da perzon dat is oplning 2 pt da stry on hr akont, do fukn dar,it ix my fukn stry, nt urz. Gt it?!?!!?

Chapter 21: Chapter 21

AN: Sop fmaing me u prepz!!!!!11 Raven, dizx 1s u!!!!11111 MRC ROXS!!!!!!!!

XXXXXXX666ZXXXXXXX

"OMS" I fukn yled. "Y da fuk id u jond doz prepz. Volmevort tryd 2 kil u, u fukn dumhed"

"By he fretnd 2 kil u", Draco sed.

"Dats ok", I sed senaly 2 hm.

"Hw u fukn der do dat", yled da otha Def Deelet. "U wil b punshd wif def" c tuk her masl of, & it wuz dat fukn slut Paris.

"I dona fukn kiil u fukn btch", I yled secily.

"U cnt, cuz im Stanist!!!!!!!!!!1111", c cremd.

"No u nt, u r fukn posr. Inly goffz cn b satnizt!!!!!!!!!!!1111", I fukn pizd ut!!!!!!!!!!11111111.

"Voldermrf tlz da rulz arund her nw, u fukn no gud goff. 4 nw on, all goffz will DI!!!!!!!!!11111", dat fukn pser yld. I cudnt believ it, I cudnt b a goff animor. I wnted to go & slt my rits, & listnd 2 sum MCR& sum Ritez of sprng, bt I nu I hd 2 sumfing abut Parid. So I did a spll, bt c blikd it.

"Wat da fuk", I yled!!!!!!!!!!11

"Us prepz hav da powr of Voldesnort, so u cunt defet me, u fukn goff!!!!!!!!11"

I wuz so fukn pizzd da I cud nt tak it. Sudnly, c hite me wif a blot of gren lite. I wuz ded...............

XXXXXXXXXxx

AN: Wuz dat better?!?

THE END

My Immortal 2: Fangz 4 De Venom

Chapter 1.

AN: dis iz da reel seqwel to My Immortal, k? fangz (get it? Cuz I'm goffick and a vampire?) to my new frend Xanthan Gum, hu is also my nu beata. Fangz lso 4 leting me use yur OOOC. Ur so awsum, its liek raven came bak an now has a kok!

XXXXXXXXXXXXXXXXXXXXXXXXXXXXXXXXXXXXX666XXXXXXXXXXXXXXXXXXXXXXXXXXXXX XXXXXXXXXXXX

The spell bounced hamlessly against Volzemorte's robes. He ten laffed in a preppy way.

"hahaha" he laughed knowingly "Is that the bst thou can doeth?" He then raised something above his hed, which from where me, Vampire, Draco, Diabolo and B'Loody Mary stood appeared to be a popsickle stik shaped lik a tampon.

"Now thou shalt all dieth" he said, raising the apparatus above him so sexily I nearly wet myself. Vampire and Draco cried fevently. Diabolo ran off suicidally. B'Loody Mary began slitting her wrists. I grasped.

And then...................we heard a noise!1 a dud apeered and waived a torch in Valdemoore's fece. "bak!!111 Bac, beast!1 I warned ya!" he shooted angrily. Then sum wind blew, and his torch got jiggy wit it before it became smoke. Volsimoret looked fearful as he blue away.

"Fangz for saving us" I said to the nucumer. He was a tall 47-yo man with pale skin, but not so pail that I could tell he was not a vampire or a

zombie (the later of whik reminds of the goffick rocker and his gofvick wife). His eyes were a succulent blue color that I instantly lost myself in. His hair was short and a brownish blonde colour, and he had a short beard that was starting to white. He wore a blak tshirt with red stitch markings at the hems. On the shirt, it read, in blood red coloring "U got Brick-rolled" on the front and "Goff 4 lyf" on teh back. A pear of denim blue jeans covered his waste and legs, with a small leather tag that sed "Levi's". He had on blue socks and some white tennis shoes with red markings on them. The laces were an offwhite color, so that they looked almost like string cheese shreds that were starting to get mouldy.

He slimed at me "NP. My name is Brickbuilder Robert Zanganese Portuguese Siamese Lebanese Chinese Japanese Cantonese Thollerson, but you can call me Brick or Bob the Builder." *(Xan dis is u!111)* He then pulled out a stick of butter and began eating it in a goffick way.

"Du yu go to Hogwartz?" I asked. "Yah, I got there at the start of term. I rode up on a mystical unicorn that only I look cool riding on. Her name was Butterscotch, and she had a horn made of butter!1"

"Well, I'm in Slitherin House, u?"

Brick then did a dance that consisted of jumping around like he was on both the E and the X taken between 'the crack'. Wen he ended this ritul, he said "i'm in Hufflepuff, which is yellow like butter! And there's all u can eat butter tha! R u coming with me?"

I thought about it for a while, then nodded.

"Enoby, we have to get back to the castle!11" B'Loody Mary shrieked.

"Go, I'll ketchup with you l8r, bich" I said annoyedly.

She cried tearz of blood and ran off with Vampire and Draco who were still crying tears of blood from earlier.

"Lets go, bitch!" Brick said moodily as he hippy skipped to the castle. I followed.

Chapter 2.

A/N: Prepz, stup falamine the stolry, if u dnot liker it, then fukc of!11 U kante like sumting until u tired it!111 Fangz to Xanthan Gum 4 helpeing me writer tis chaperter.

XXXXXXXXXXXXXXXXXXXXXXXXXXXXXXXXXXXX666XXXXXXXXXXXXXXXXXXXXXXXXX
XXXXXXXXXXXXX

When we gut to the Hufflepufr commen ruum, Brick ran over to tha frigerator and got out lots of stix of butter. He used his goffick eyes to melt the butter into glasses that he gave 2 us 2 drink. He drank about 47 glasses, his age. We talked l8 in2 the nite, and agreed to visit Dumbleydored's office the next day.

I went to my coffin later that niet and closed the lid to sleep. I looked over at Willow's coffin next to mine, wishing that she hadn't taken a steak to the heart earlier. At leest she was in immortal goffick now.

The next moening, I went to the gargoyle outside Dumbeldure's artifice, when suddenly, I saw Brick standing in the corner. He was eating something sexily. I aproched him.

"Brick!11 WTF r u doing? I asked.

"I jUsT 8 SuM cHiCkEn McNuGgEtS!!!1" he said in a stiletto voice.

"alrighte, we need to get past this garley" I seid to him.

"Alou me' Brick said, tuning to face the stature. "stik of buttr!" he shoted. Butt nothing hapend!11 "Stix of butte4r!" he tried agen! And nuthting happened! "47 sticks of butr!" he screemed.

Just then, Vampire cummed over to us. "Let me' he said angrily. "Tub of marg-"

Brick got all violent then, and his eyes flashed a goffik red color as he began stupinating him. "Don't say that word around me, motherfucker!11" he shouted sadly!1

Then a figure wearing a black robe approached us. He was wearing a black robe made of cotton. His shoes clackled against the soft floor. He moved over to the gargoyle, which trembled be4 him.

Margarine!

The door opened. Brick began another assault. He talked the strangr to the floor, where his hood fell off!!!!1 It was Vaultkeeper!1111

"Voltemirt!" I screamed.

"Your Mom!" Brick shouted happily *(that's Brick's name for Volzemonte)*

Dubledre then came out. He looked around and saw the fight.

Rite then, I was feeling suicidal. "Fite it, Eboby!1!1" Gandalf said to me in a cherry-flavored voice. But I kudn't any longer. I just wanted 2 take out my cut to blade myself.

"I shalt have mine revengeth noweth!" Vlitman said, ready to kill us all.

Chapter 3. Getting To Know Brick.

A fuckin' N: Hello, everybody (especially Goths and Goffz). I am Xanthan Gum, Tara's beta and (as of the other day) BF. Like Tara, I am a goth, but am not into Devil worship (instead, I worship Atheias, the Greek god of apathy). Tara has not been feeling well the past few days, but she asked me to continue her fic during her absence. Before we begin, I'd like to point out a few things. First, I beta read Tara's work before she posts it on the site, so when you flame her, you're also flaming me. Stop it, prepz! Also, this chapter will be Brick-centric (meaning it will be written in Brick's POV) so you can get to know Brick better. Okay, that's it from me. Enjoy, and if you dare flame, I'll flame you back!

XXXXXXXXXXXXXXXXXXXXXXXXXXXXXXXXGoffick_ButterXXXXXXXXXXXXXXXXXXXX
XXXXXXXXXXXX

Your Mom held his candy cane above his head as he prepared to mutter out the words that would seal our doom. Ebony was struggling to overcome the urge to cut herself (and couldn't because she had no knives with which to cut herself). Meanwhile, Dumblefucker stood helplessly at the doorway and everybody else had run off.

But I was seething with rage. Your Mom had said the M-word! I was so pissed off! How dare that fuckin' asshole say such a thing in my presence! Of course, Dumbass was also to blame – he was the one who set the flippin' password to be that unspeakable word. I wanted to kick his fuckin' ass, but not before I had dealt with Your Mom.

"Your Mom, why are you so cruel?" I asked.

"Because, little Bobby, I am –"

"It's 'Bob the Builder', asshole!" I shouted.

"Whatever. I shalt kill all thine friends and then go destroy all the butter

in the castle!"

"The fuck you will!" I shouted before tackling him to the ground. He then got up and left, his arms bleeding in a preppy way.

"Are you alright, Ebony?" I asked as I pulled her up. She nodded, and I stared into her goffick red eyes. I felt something then, or rather, some things. One I felt in my chest. The other, in my pants. Could it be that I was falling in love with someone thirty years my junior? Could there be love between a 47-year old and a 17-year old?

"Well done, Brickbuilder!" Dumbledore said as he approached.

"Hey, man, I gotta ask you something. Why the fuck do we have 'I can't believe it's not butter!' at the breakfast table, or lunch or dinner? Because I can definitely believe it's not butter!" I asked angrily.

"We do that because the school needs more funding, you son of a bitch!" Dumbledwarf said as he skipped away.

I growled in anger. "C'mon, Ebony, let's go," I said as she began dragging me off to the great hall.

When we got there, all the other students were eating, including Vampire, Diabolo, Draco, and B'Loody Mary.

"You fuckers! Why didn't you help us outside Dumbledore's office?" Ebony asked angrily.

"Yeah!" I joined in.

"Well, I got scared," Draco said.

"And we got hungry!" said everyone else.

Well, we sat down and began eating lunch. I took a hot roll, but as soon as I saw the yellow spreading substance, I knew it wasn't butter. It wasn't even 'I can't believe it's not butter!'. It was that gawdawful excuse of a spread that couldn't even hold a butter knife to butter!

"**DUMBLEFUCKER!!!**" I shouted as loudly as I could (which was just as loud as a howler), feeling fully infuriated. Just then, the delivery owls came and dropped the mail onto the students. A newspaper hit me on the head. I unrolled it and read it. My face fell at the sight of the headline:

United States President-Elect Barack Obama spends Christmas in Hawaii with the Troops

Ebony could see the anger in my goffick eyes. "What's wrong, Brick?" she asked.

"How the fuck did Barack Obama, John McCain, and Ralph Fuckin' Nader do better than a stick of butter?! We wouldn't be in this mess if the freakin' people had just voted for the butter!" I said, getting up because I was too angry to remain seated. "I'm goin' for a walk!" I said as I stormed out.

I didn't see it, but Ebony got up and followed me. We went into the Forbidden Forest together.

XXXXXXXXXXXXXXXXXXXXXXXXXXXXXXXXXXXGoffick_ButterXXXXXXXXXXXXXXXXXXXX XXXXXXXXXXXX

*There. Done. **Now review, fuckers!***

Chapter 4.

A/N: Hey, it's Xanthan Gum again. Just writing another chapter for Tara's story. I showed her the previous chapter, and she was very pleased with it! :) I'm a lucky guy to have a GF like her, even though I have a man-crush on my OC. Anyway, same deal as last chapter: enjoy, or I'll do unto you what you do to me (it's a little thing called the Golden Rule). And it's still in Brick's POV.

XXXXXXXXXXXXXXXXXXXXXXXXXXXXXXXGoffick_ButterXXXXXXXXXXXXXXXXXXXX
XXXXXXXXXXXX

We went deep into the Forbidden Forest. By this time, I was aware that Ebony had been following me, and that I was no longer mad at Dumbledore. Though the incident in the great hall still filled my heart with hate. I knew I had to act quickly – the school's supply of butter wouldn't last long against Your Mom and his followers. But I still had time.

"Brick?" Ebony asked. "Are you okay?"

"Yeah."

"If you don't mind me asking, why do you call Voldemort 'Your Mom'?"

I took out a stick of butter and began munching on it, talking between mouthfuls. "Well, Ebony, you see – (munch, munch) – some time ago, he came to me in a dream – (Oh, damn, that's good butter, I hope it never runs out) – and said "I'm Your Mom!" – (crunch, crunch) – and the name stuck. Fuck, that's good butter!" I said as I popped the last morsel of the stick into my waiting mouth. It felt good going down.

Right then, we heard some rustling in the bushes, which scared us.

"Brick! What was that?" Ebony asked me in a concerned voice.

"I don't know, but I just melted some butter in my pants," I said. Indeed,

the crotch of my blue jeans had become discolored with moisture – which happens when I either forget I have sticks of butter in my pockets, or I wet myself. I don't know which applied in this case. It didn't matter, though, because at that very moment in time, a creature appeared. It was a man from the navel up, and a horse from there down. It was a centaur!

"Ew, gross, Brick!" Ebony said disgustedly at my last comment.

"Peace, strangers," the centaur greeted. "I am Firenze."

"I'm calling you Cenarius," Ebony said while seductively blinking her eyelids. I pretty much got a hard-on from the sight.

"...Right, well, I'll be going now," the centaur formerly known as Firenze said as he dashed off into the forest's depths.

"What a fucking prep!" I said, noting how Ebony's style made him uncomfortable – a characteristic of how a prep acts in the presence of esteemed goffz like ourselves.

"I couldn't agree more!" Ebony said. We stared into each other's eyes, noting how goffik they appeared. Unconsciously, we moved towards each other, the only sound being the owls hooting as the sun shone through the branches of the trees (though there was very little light at all).

We wound up making cream-of-us soup. Plain and simple. Unless you don't get my drift, in which case you are a prep!

Chapter 5.

A/N: Hey, it's Xanthan Gum here once again. I showed Tara my previous chapter late last night, and she was also pleased with my output. She is quickly getting better, so this'll probably be the last chapter that I fill in for, at least for a while. Once more, I'll remind you preps to mind your place if you know what's best for you. That said, we'll have one more chapter in Brick's POV (at least for a while).

XXXXXXXXXXXXXXXXXXXXXXXXXXXXXXXXXGoffick_ButterXXXXXXXXXXXXXXXXXXX
XXXXXXXXXXXX

It was late afternoon when we finally got our nude selves out from under the linen blanket we had shared as we got on our clothes and packed up our makeshift camp. By this time, classes had ended for the day, but Ebony and I didn't care. Ebony didn't care about the classes, and I didn't either, because we're both goffick like that. That, and Ebony's a vampire as opposed to a full-on witch, and I'm hiding a dark secret from her. No, I'm not going to tell you because then you'll tell Ebony, and my dark secret wouldn't be so dark or secret anymore now, would it? Oh, and don't tell her I have a dark secret, either. That would be bad. For me.

Anyway, we went back to the castle. We hung out in the Slytherin Common Room with Draco and a fine-lookin' piece of adolescent tail named Pansy Parkinson. Ebony calls her Pansy. I could go either way, if you know what I mean (wink).

Soon, it was time to go to dinner. I was hesitant at first, because I still remembered the incident in the great hall a few hours earlier. But Ebony promised me it wouldn't be so bad this time. On top of that, Pansy would be going with us, so we went without hesitation. In retrospect, dinner wasn't as bad as I thought, mostly because there was

finally (emphasis on that word) butter at the table! I was so happy that if Dumbledore was standing near me, I would have Italianed him (it's like Frenching, except it's Italian in origin) in a heartbeat (and he would've done the same since he's a faggot).

After dinner, me, Ebony, Draco, and Pansy got into Draco's car and flew to Hogsmeade because we'd heard that Beloved Enemy was playing there. When we got there, we paid for some tickets and picked out some seats. The lead singer took the stage, and Ebony got wet at the crotch because he was so goffick.

"*Damn you, get outta my head! You are my endless disease. Die if you can, if you please. Damn you, get outta my head! Kill me, she lingers on and on. How dare they forbid it, my virus undead!*" he sang as the crowd swayed to the beat.

I screamed while eating a stick of butter and waving my buttery hands in the air wildly. As the band finished and got off stage, I slipped past security and got on stage, where I did a dance like as though I was on both the E and the X taken between 'the crack' before I took the microphone and announced, "Ebony Dark'ness Dementia Raven Way, there's something I realized since the other day — I love you!"

Ebony gasped, but I couldn't see it clearly, nor could I hear it. But I touched her, and that was enough for me as security handed me over to the police, who then quote-unquote "took me into custody".

Chapter 6.

AN: K, Im bak, pplz! I wuznt felling gud l8ly, but now im fin. Fangz to XG 4 helping me wid the last feu chaptrs. I liek ur work!!1

XXXXXXXXXXXXXXXXXXXXXXXXXXXXXXXXXX666XXXXXXXXXXXXXXXXXXXXXXXX XXXXXXXXXXXXX

I went 2 bed melancholily thet nigt b-cuz theyd tachen Brick 2 Azerbaijan. Eye tried to sleep, but I miszd Brick two much. So............I didn't't sleep at all that nit. But something eels existad that I couldnot shape out. Why arest Brick?

"Becuse Brick poped your cherry for teh six hundred sixty sixth time, Enoby!" Dumbledorea said to me in the dreem I was having awake!!1111

"I'm not a slute!1" I shouted, but then I
...fell asleep.

The nxt mrnng, I slunked in2 Dubledures officina (I tot u the Spnish word for office) and found sum flu power. I used it 2 teleport too Asskissban. The gards there smled me and gav me sum hot coco.

"R u here 2 c Brick?" the warden asked me. I noded.

Brick was in a cell. It was small from da looks of itl.

"Ebodgy, im glad to se u!1" he.

The head wyvern forked him with a clib. "Nu talking to strangurs!" shouted.

"But I no her!!!!11111111"Brick sweated.

"Okay" the varren said signing off.

"So im here" I spooned sexily.

"Okay, Ebondy, I need u to du me a favor" Brick said, getting out a stick of butr. "Ineedutogreasethebarsandmybodytoletmeouttahere" Brick said so fast that I kud barley understand him. So I greased those and he was free. We stalked back to the castle.

Chapter 7.

AN: It's XG again. Tara wanted to post one more chapter before the New Year, but feels too depressed to write, so I'll fill in for her once again. I assume that you've figured it out by now that when Tara writes, it's from the POV of Ebony, and since I'm writing, it'll be Brick's POV. Okay, enjoy, and no fuckin' flamers!

XXXXXXXXXXXXXXXXXXXXXXXXXXXXXXXXGoffick_ButterXXXXXXXXXXXXXXXXXXX
XXXXXXXXXXX

Ebony and I ran until we were back at the castle. I was a free man again! I'd done nothing wrong, so that proves how big of preps the law enforcement peoples are. But we had no time to celebrate. I wanted to know how someone knew I was to be arrested, and Your Mom was still out there somewhere, plotting something diabolical. I had to save myself and the school's supply of butter!

We sent Pansy to talk with Dumbledore about expunging my criminal record. Then, Ebony went off to Dumbledark's office to feed! And then I went to Dumbledork's office to see if there was any butter left in the kitchens. This is what it all boiled down to:

- My criminal record had been righteously expunged;

- Dumbledord was well on his way to becoming a vampire (and not just any vampire – a gay vampire!)

- There was still butter in the kitchen, which is where I needed to go next.

We went towards the kitchen area, where we saw that preppy painting of a fruit bowl. Ebony tried eating the fruited canvas. Pansy touched her cherry. I rubbed my pickle.

Then the elf known as Dobby came and tickled the fuckin' pear. The painting swung aside to allow us entrance to the kitchens. I then did what I always do: I ate all the butter, then blamed it on Dumblefucker and Your Mom.

"**DUMBLEFUCKER!!! YOUR MOM!!!**" I screamed angrily.

"Nice going, asshole!" Dumbledumb chided. I was so pissed off, I dunked Dobby into a pot of boiling water. He died, and nobody would know (except for me) that stewed house elf would be on the menu for the next meal. The other house elves panicked and fled in terror.

"I'm not a terrorist!" I shouted. Really, I'm not. I just get angry sometimes. But the stupid elves wouldn't listen.

I found a few pieces of parchment on a counter, left there rather conspicuously. It was evidence! It chronicled how Lupin and Snape had found a new accomplice in their heinous perversion. It was the midget, Flitwick!

I decided to take an oath right then and there. "By my hand, Your Mom will die!"

Chapter 8.

AN: Prupz, donut flame dis chapter its importont 2 me!1 Fangz tu XG 4 da help.

XXXXXXXXXXXXXXXXXXXXXXXXXXXXXXXXXXX666XXXXXXXXXXXXXXXXXXXXXXXX XXXXXXXXXXXXX

We kwikly left da kitchens. Brock had maed a huge mess. And Dumbeldore was lying dead on fleur.

We now had a leak. Panty did some stuff, and soon we wur hot on da trale of midgetman!

XXXXXXXXXXXXXXXXXXXXXXXXXXXXXXXXXXX666XXXXXXXXXXXXXXXXXXXXXXXX XXXXXXXXXXXXX

I no itz short, but Im sad dat 2008 is gawne!

Chapter 9. Bang The Doldrums.

AN: Prips, dnot mocha me! Dis iz not a joek! Im sere-us! N no flaming either!

XXXXXXXXXXXXXXXXXXXXXXXXXXXXXXXXXXXX666XXXXXXXXXXXXXXXXXXXXXXXXX
XXXXXXXXXXXXX

As we wur running down da core and door, Brick suddently stopped. "It's time 4 my dayly cuttin' session" he sed deliciously. We joined him and cut our selves, after which I made sum roonds to suck every1's blud. We then résuméd our chase. Not long after, tho, Brick saw a newsstand. He shoped to reed an paper. This is the hedline he saw.

Barack Obama sworn in as 44th President of United States; Joe Biden ascends to Vice Presidency

Right then, Brick-Bob's eyes began twitching and glowing with the passion of a woman touching herself when she's all alone, but Brick's a man so he woodnot note ice, u dunderheaded prepz. He was flaming mad!1 (no, not like u, prpex) He looked liek he was about to shit a brick!111!1

"Butter wsa supposed 2 win!11111 I'm so fuckin' mad right now, I could shit a brick!11" shitted B.K. Broiler®.

"Brick, we have 2 go!12" I said angrily.

"Come cum, we can all go 2 McDnlds" said Cerebral Palsy. So we all went gaily.

"I fEeL sO fUcKiN' sUiCiDaL!" Brick said after eating 666 McCains (geddit, cuz im goffick and a santaist!). We were almist dune mrunchig when Vozemor showed up!11111111111!!!!!1

"We have no tme 4 u!" Pransye shooted, but General Grievous wouldn't take no for an anwar. He chased down and chopped to pieces!111

"OMG!!1" I screamed.

There lie Yaxley, who had been filling in fore Vladimir who was presently having sum muggle whore clean off hiser manly clock (c, opreps? I said that and not u-no-wot! Im not as immature as u sai – im all growed up!11)

"Oh...............

...

...

...

...

...

...

...

...

...

...

...

...

...

...

...

...

...

...

...

...

...

...

...

...

...

...

...
...
...
...
...
...
...
...
...
...
...
...
...
...
...
...
...
...
...
...
...
...
...
...
...
...
...
...
...
...
...
...

MY IMMORTAL

MY IMMORTAL

..
..
..
..
..
..
..
..
..
..
..
..
..
..
..
..
..
..
..
..
..
..
..
..
..
..
..
..
..
..
..
..

MY IMMORTAL

..
..
..
..
..
..
..
..
..
..
..
..
..
..
..
..
..
..
..
..
..
..
..
..
..
..
..
..
..
..
..
..
..
..
..

...
...pity.....................................
...
...
...
...
...
...
...
...
...
...
...
...
...
...
...
...
...
...
...
...
...
...
...
...
...
...
...
...
...
...
...

...
...
...
...
...
...
...
...
...
...
...
...
...
...
...
...
...
...
...
...
...
...
...
...
...
...
...
...
...
...
...
...
...
...
...
...

...
...
...
...
...
...
...
...
...
...
...
...

...” said chief musketeer and head chef Goron Romstein, lead singer of the goffick band Rammstein. He then cut his throat, and Yaxley died!!!1

“OMFG!” cried Gordon Brown as he took out a razor blade to kill the outgoing president of the Union for America.

“I’m on it” secluded Jack Bower of the preppy show 28 *(did u no thot’s the drinking age in Zimbabweasel!?)*.

2 B Cntnu’d…

Chapter 10.

An: OMG, wut do u preps wunt from me?/ Y cont u shut up an stup beng prepz?!1 Fangsz 2 XG fer teh help. Im glade u licked it!111

XXXXXXXXXXXXXXXXXXXXXXXXXXXXXXXXXXXXX666XXXXXXXXXXXXXXXXXX
XXXXXXXXXXXXXXXXXXX

Ass the day wore on, we all grew tired of our pursuit of the perverted midget and decided to call it a day wasted on chasing a petrified, overgrown gnome. We returned to the castle happily. Brick left us as we went into the Slytherin Common Room. Just as I was about to start getting ready for bed, Draco entered. He was wearing a black leather unitard with the words "Im gotik, you motherfucking prepz!" *(an: I wish*

Hot Topik had tis shrit caus den I could sho it off 2 u prepz!) He was also wearing four laced shoues and a lot of black eyeliner. He looked exactly like Cheaster Bannigton *(if u don't know who heis, get teh fuek outta hiya!).*

"Hey, Enoby! Wanna see a gotfick concert 2nite?" he asked.

"Yeah, why not?" I rippled.

"C'mon, I have the car all warmed up!1"

We went out into the car and flew all the way to Hogsmeade where all the concerts are held. There was Linking Parker, and Good Charlotte with hints of MCR.

I was so hot to see the static *(an: geddits? Cause Im gothicek and a Satinist!11111)* lineup, I began running around like a little baby does before it can learn to break the law. Unfortunately, we learned of a terrible accident down the rod.

"My friends, Likin Part had a terrible accident down the rod!!!!!1" screamed Mike Shinindoah, who has such goffick almond-eyes. "Every member of the band is tombly injured!" *(an: I spruked up da language, cause evry1 sez gavelly)* "But MCR will cover their song 'Valentine's Day'".

"OMFG!" I screamed haafhartedly. I wanted to saw the members of LIP (cause theire Lying In Pieces, like in one of their songs *(if u dont know which sung, ill kill u stupid prep! I noe where u live!)* But I love MCR, so I stayed for them. Gerard Way is so hot anyway!1

So now you're gone

And I was wrong

I never knew what it was like to be alone

On Valentine's Day! On Valentine's Day! Sang Gerard's sexy as ever voice.

After the show, I discovered th Draco left wihtou me!11

I was pissed until I heard Gerard make a post-season announcement: "I'll take one lucky girl from the audience...................................you!" he pointed at me!

"Yes, you!"

I nervesly went on stage as everyone else left us in pieces (once more, prepz...I no voodoo!! Boogey woogey woogey!1)

Well, we met up and talked about stuff and then went to grab some food. Eventully, we crawled into the same bed as mine (it was mine, or R u 2 stoopid to undermine that?!) naked!!! He wastreled no time in putting his boy-twiggie in me girl hole!11

"Enboy, I wanna telly ou some good news!" Gerard said.

"What is it?"

"It's so good, I'll tell now!"

"What the fuck is it?"

"We're DNA-related!"

I cried, realizing that almost all of my most goffick off gotfrick dreams was cumming *(geddit cause I slept with my brother Gerard in sex?)* torture.

I slept till the next morning when...................................

"I GOT YOU NOW! ILL TELL THIS TO DUMBLEDORE, YOU SKUNK!"

It was...Sexmidget!

XXXXXXXXXXXXXXXXXXXXXXXXXXXXXXXXXXXX666XXXXXXXXXXXXXXXXXXXXXXXXX
XXXXXXXXXXXXX

Wuz it guud, darling? Plz reveiow, or I won't post again till I get tweety good 1s!!1

Chapter 11.

AN: OK, I haf a feu anoncments 2 make. Furst, I changled my SN cause I lyke the new 1 betr. Also, I'm going to vacation in da place wher they movied "Twilite" for a few days, so XG will fill in 4 mie. Speeking of the devil (getdit, cause I'm Stanaistic!), he will write 4 my behalve. Fangz, Xan-man! Ad no flaming, preps, or I be mad!!!1

XXXXXXXXXXXXXXXXXXXXXXXXXXXXXXXXXXXXX666XXXXXXXXXXXXXXXXXXXXXXXXXX XXXXXXXXXXXXX

I looked from Gerard's dead-hot body to the midgeted young man, who was wearing russet-colored robes and a black hood cause he wanted to be a gothik pervert. The room was silent as the diminutively demonic

(geddit?) Profesor Flitwick stood over us. He keep shuting about how he was going to get us expelled from Hogwarts. Suddenly the door opened.

"OMFG, this is hot!" Lopekin stated as he entered, with Snocone cumming from behind *(getit, cause he's a fang and hes in love with Loumpkin)* "Nice going, Flitmin!"

"They're not supposed to know about us!" Flimmaker said angstilly.

"Oh, it's ok, they use the same brand of condems as us!" Snapple added fruiticiously. "Besides, you were the last to join us, and that was because we described how good you are at being a perverted little super-midget!"

"Stop that pigmy-crap!" shrieked Fleetweek.

"What? You may be small, but your assets aren't so!1" replied roomilus.

"I didn't mean to"

The door opened again and McGottagal came in with Dumbledore. She was wearing a black long-sleeve shirt with a sterling silver necklace and a brown ankle-length skirt. Dumbledore was wearing purple robes that had little yellow stars on them that looked like pentagrams. Thei walked over to all of us and got mad! "OMFG, what hte flying **FUCK** is going on here?!" Dumbbelldork screamed so loudly that his voice could be recorded and used to make a howler.

"You should be ashamed of all your selves! You've all single-handedly rooned the Hogwarts tradition and experience! I'm going to report this to Conrelius Fruitopia!" McCockle shriek'd.

She was about to move when a clicking noise was herd and that was when she noticed that something had gotten under her skuht. "I see Lomedome, I see Frants, I see sexy ass-panties!" called Flitperv's voiceover.

"EEEP!" she crief as she lifted up her red skirt to let the poivoited little

person out (he was carrying a camera shaped like a dildo). She raised it so hi that we could all see her wearing some white satin *(an: it's almost spelled like Satan, lol)* panties with a picture of a large maryjewwana leaf on the crotch. Gerard fainted, the three bumbling perverts began working the mechanics of the nether reijons, and Dumbledore gasped as he looked on at the miracle.

"Mini-rova, I didn't know you wore those! It almost makes me want to become str8!1"

"Then do so, and be quick about it!" she repleated, and soon the two parents were Frenching pacifically. Eventually, they smiled while breaking apart.

"Everyone, I declare this day to be Great National Bisexual Love Day!" Dumbledore shouted gothically. The two lovers almost litrally kicked me and Gerard out of bed so that they cold get it on themselves. Last I saw of them, they wee crawling under the covers and cloves were going airborne. Gerard cauth the panties and put thim on 2 hide his manlioness, which made me sad and hot at the same time.

I was angry, but at that moment, the whole place shook like there were earthquakes in the house.

Thumple- Thumple- Thumple- Thumple

"OMFG, the house is falling apart!" Gerard cried out as he suddenly came too. We were about to open the door but it banged!

BANG! The door went.

Suddenly it opened and Hairgriddy entered slowly, rubbing his head as he got up (he had to crawl thru the doorway cause he's so small for a giant). He rose till his head hit the ceiling cause he's so tall for a man. He began lion-roaring some stuff.

"OMFG, ENOBYU, I BUMPED HEAD ON DOOR CAUSE I FORGOT HOW OPEN DOOR AND I PAID PRICE FOR IT! THEN I HIT HEAD ON SEALING

CAUSE I FORGOT HOW TALL I AM!!!1 I COME NOW 2 SAVE YOU N THAT FUCKING SEXY GUY NEXT 2 YOU IN MOST GOFFIX WAY TRANSPIRABLE!111 *(AN: Hagrrid is bi, and is hot b/c of that)*"

"But Hargid, I don't need 2 B saved!" I protesticled.

"Yeah, giant man-dude!" Gerard multiplied.

"YUO DON'T UNDERSTAND! WE NEED 2 LIEIVE NOW! IT NOT SAFE HERE ANYMORE! IT VERY DANGEROUS NOW! SO WE MUST LEAVFE WHILE WE STEEL CAN *(Geddit, cause I like metal)*! **JIF WE DNOT LEAVE NOW, THERE WILL BE SERIOUS CENSORSHIPS! LEAVE WITH ME, AND WE MIGHT LIVE 2 C 2MORROW! BUT IF YOU DNOTY, THEN VLACKMORTE WILL COME TO CHASE YOU DOWN HACK 2 PIECES! AND AS 4 U, MAN-CANDY, HE WILL SEND HIS DETH DEALERS TO DEAL W/ YOU!1 THEY DEAL IN DEATH AND WILL SELL IT 2 U REAL CHEAP, BUT YOU WON'T WANT 2 BUY IT! I KNOW YOU WANNA LIVE, UNLYEK EBONDY, BUT DEATH WILL COME 4 U IF U DON'T CUM W/ ME THIS INSTANT! I NOT KIDDING! WE MUST RUSH OUT THIS HOUSE OR THEY FIND YOU AND MAKE U SIT IN CHEAP CHEAP CHAIR AND DRINK DRINK DEEPLY THE POWDER OF THE ELUSIVE ELIXER OF DEATH!1111 LEAVE NOW, WE MUST! IT ONLY WAY WE SURVIVE!"**

Well, we left the place evilly cause if we didn't ten we woodn't be Satanistas now, would we, prepz? We got onto Hackrid's black Skullbolt 2008 (he sold the bike and used da $money$ 4 da broomstock) and he started it up. Soon, we were in the sky. However, a problem soon came up.

"WE SEEM TO HAVE SOME EXTRA GOFFICK W8! WE NEED TO ALL GO ON GOFFIK ANOREXIA DIETS OR WE WILL SURELY LAND-CRASH!1"

I looked down and was sexy to find that that cute little pervert was clinging onto my robes. I lifted him and realized he looked exactly like my infant child.

"Baby want sum milk?" I asked, taking of my shit and bar. He began

suckling away sexily.

"WE GONNA CRASH!1!!1" Hargrid warned as we began a notsosubtle crashing!

Following the crash-impacting on the ground outside of a palace described to my be Hairigrid as Beauxbatons, I realized just how much I missed my Brick-roller, my Vampire, and my blonde bubble-headed bitch boy.

XXXXXXXXXXXXXXXXXXXXXXXXXXXXXXXXXX666XXXXXXXXXXXXXXXXXXXXXXXXXXX XXXXXXXXXXXX

Lungest 1 yet 4 dis chaptie! K, da next group of stuffs is all u, babe! Luv ya!1 We shood get it on weselves sumtime soon!

-TG

Chapter 12.

*A/N: It's Xanthan Gum again! Remember me? I know it's been a while, cause Tara's done most of the writing since the last time I wrote, but I've been proofreading her works to her greatest satisfaction. I'm upset that some of you preps are still flaming her – **CUT IT OUT!!!** It's not funny! How would you like it if someone flamed one of your fics?! Huh?! Anyway, we're back in Brick's POV, and as a sidenote, Tara and I now both own the profile, and I've added my stuff to Tara's. Damn, I love that woman! I agree, we should work the mechanics sometime soon! I'm currently planning a trip to Victoria's Secret in preparation for that! What do you want? Scented candles, goffick lingerie, a vibrator, what? Thanks!*

XXXXXXXXXXXXXXXXXXXXXXXXXXXXXXXXGoffick_ButterXXXXXXXXXXXXXXXXXXXXXXX XXXXXXXXXXXX

Well, I was stuck in the boy's dormitory of the Hufflepuff wing of the castle. Ebony was gone somewhere, and it had been a few days since last I saw her. This left me without a sense of fullness. It got so bad that I had to resort to doin' what I'm doin' right now: masturbating. Somehow, once you've lost your virginity, whackin' off doesn't feel as good anymore. Am I right, fellow goffz, or amirite? Prepz, you don't get to answer cause you're all still virgins and always will be, so you'd never be able to truthfully answer this question.

Anyway, it was time for me to be leavin' the dormitory and head down to the great hall for some good ol'-fashioned food. En route, I ran into Ernie MacMillan (or as I call him, "The Mac", and whenever he comes to me with confidence issues, I tell him that he'll always be far better than John McCain, who is not worthy of the title "Mac" (and who righteously lost…but not to butter! GRRRRRRRRRRRRRRRR!). Indeed, only "The Mac" and "Mac"Donald's are worthy of the prestigious title).

"Hey, Brick!" The Mac greeted. "Listen, um, there's this big dance coming up real soon in Hogsmeade, and I wanna ask this really hot chick from Ravenclaw to go with me, but I don't know how to ask her. What should I say?"

I smirked before replying. Ever since becoming a goff, The Mac has had more ladies to fuck than any other guy, even guys older than him. Girls practically line up to be his next girlfriend, even if all they want is a pity-fuck. Because of this, he has become one of my best friends besides Ebony and her group of super-best friends. But now was the time to be replyin' to my friend's plea.

"Well, The Mac, simply take this to heart: You are now, and always will be, far better than John McCain. Tell her this, and she'll never wanna hang with any other guy besides you."

"Wow, thanks, Brick! I'm goin' to tell her that right away!" he thanked, then ran out.

Meanwhile, I continued to the great hall. Though the air smelled

delicious enough to eat, I was not pleased by the menu. Stuffed liver, sushi, steamed vegetables, mincemeat pie... it wouldn't fill for me. So I left the area (much to the disappointment of my fellow Hufflepuff goffz, but I see them all the time in the common room anyway) and instead went to the campus McDonald's for dinner (yes, there is a McDonald's on the Hogwarts campus, or did you stupid preps not read that part of the story?). Once there, I ate several chicken McNuggets with several glasses of Coke (the drug, not the soda). I wAs DeBaTiNg WhEtHeR tO gEt ThOsE oR a FiLeT-o-FiSh SaNdWiCh *(A/n: HeRe, FiShY, fIsHy, FiShY...cOmE hErE, cOmE hErE...cOmE tO fUcKiN' pApA sO i CaN kIlL yOu, GuT yOu, ScAlE yOu, SkIn YoU, dEeP-fRy YoU, pLaCe YoU oN a StEaMeD bUn AnD eAt YoU!!!)*

LaTeR tHaT nIgHt, I wAs In FoR a ReAl TrEaT bEcAuSe ThE mAc WaS gOiN' tO aSk ThE fInE pIeCe Of RaVeNcLaW tAiL tO tHe DaNcE. iT wAs So BeAuTiFuL tHaT i AlMoSt StArTeD wEePiN'. tHiS iS wHaT hE sAiD.

"MiNeRaLeRvA *(a/N: tHaT's ThE bItCh ThE mAc WaS aSkInG)*, i KnOw ThAt I aM nOw, AnD aLwAyS wIlL bE, mUcH bEtTeR tHaN jOhN mCcAiN. iN dArKnEsS oF tHaT, wIlL yOu Go To ToMoRrOw NiGhT's DaNcE wItH mE?"

"I dOn'T rEaLlY fUcKiN' cArE, yOu HoT pIeCe Of EyE-cAnDy! FuCk YeS!"

I nEaRlY cRiEd ThEn. As FaR aS yOuR aVeRaGe GoFf GoEs, ThE mAc WaS cOmIn' InTo HiS oWn RaThEr QuIcKlY. aLl He NeEdEd WaS sOmE gOfFiCk EnCoUrAgEmEnT, aNd I gAvE hIm ThE bAsIcS, wHiCh He MaStErEd InStAnTlY aLl By HiMsElF. iF i WeRe HeAdMaStEr Of HoGwArTs, ThEn I wOuLd DeClArE hIm ReAdY tO gRaDuAtE. hOwEvEr, I wAs StArTiNg To CoMe DoWn FrOm My HiGh, So I nEeDeD tO hIdE sO nObOdY cOuLd SeE mE wHeN i RaN oUt Of ThE mAgIc HiGh. DeFtLy, I jUmPeD bEhInD a BuSh To HiDe.

When I came out from behind the bush, my high had ended, and I felt the emptiness once again. I was about to dejectedly head to the Hufflepuff boy's dormitories when The Mac pulled me aside to thank me. We started peeing on the bush I had just hid in (that's how I thank

plants for saving my ass, and my piss is even more acidic than stomach acid!).

"Wow, Brick, your advice really worked! She said yes, so now I'm all set to acquire another STD! Wanna trade blood again?"

"Not really. I'm still fightin' off the Syphilis from your last transfusion. And there was the HPV before that."

"Okay, well, when you get better, come see me, okay?"

"Will do, The Mac! By the way, what do expect to get this time?"

"Gonorrhea, or maybe even AIDS if I'm lucky."

"For sure," I said as I finished, zipped up my pants, and slapped The Mac's ass before enterin' the castle and feelin' immensely lonely. I quickly went to the Hufflepuff common room and got naked. Then, I started to masturbate. I was a lone lion king, all alone in his domain save for one sultry and sexy mattress. I went to work and was about to start ejaculatin' all over the place when someone entered. It was Vampire.

"AAAHHH!" I screamed as I blew my load on him. He seemed almost stunned by the act, and had I not remembered Ebony tellin' me about his gay past, I would have been surprised by his calm reaction.

"...Hey, Brick. I wanted to talk to you about Ebony, but I can see that now is not a good time for that. I'll just come back later," he said as he left.

"You're damn right it's a bad time!" I shouted as I threw thirty used condoms at the now-closed door.

Then I got to thinkin' about what I had been thinkin' about earlier in the evenin', and decided that with Dumbleloser out of the way, I could name myself headmaster of Hogwarts! I would do it right now (not the sex, cause I just did it by myself)!

I left the common room as I was (fuck clothes, man!). A few people turned to look at my little stick of butter *(you know, the one guys have between the frontal part of the area where the legs connect to the body?)*, but nobody said anythin'. I guess they were all taken aback by its sheer beauty, handsomeness, and hotness. Only Mr. Norris had to complain.

"Damn my squibby eyes, why the fuck is there a student struttin' through the hallways NAKED?!"

"Mrow..."

"DON'T LOOK, FILTH, THE SIGHT OF IT WILL-"

"MEOW!"

"Too late..."

While Mr. Norris took Filth to the hospital to restore the sight to the cat's blind eyes, I continued my stroll to the headmaster's office. The statue opened automatically cause it never saw a hot and naked student body before. It was a goffik gargoyle.

Inside Dumbledore's office, all the paintin's of past headmasters and headmistresses began mumblin' angrily with each other. I think it was because they were somehow "offended" by my naked self. I was determined, however, to become both the youngest headmaster in the history of Hogwarts, and the least clothed one at that. I found a piece of parchment on the desk, on which I wrote: "**I, Brickbuilder Robert Zanganese Portuguese Siamese Lebanese Chinese Japanese Cantonese Thollerson, do hereby take the oath of the office of the Headmaster of Hogwarts School of Witchcraft and Wizardry, and will run it however I see fit.**"

I was too tired then to do anythin' official, so when it became official, I went back to the Hufflepuff dormitory. I got into my top-bunk bed (The Mac sleeps below me).

"Hey, Brick? You still awake?"

"Yeah."

"Listen, thanks again for helping me earlier."

"No sweat."

"And congratulations on becoming headmaster. What are you going to do first?"

"I was thinkin' that tomorrow, I'd get you ready to graduate, cause goffz are the smartest people in the world. You may not know this, but I heard you ask her out, and I'm convinced that there's nothing more I can teach you, cause you've already gained a mastery of anything I could ever teach you!"

"But...I don't wanna leave you!"

"You won't have to, which is why I'll make it so that exceptional students such as yourself can continue to live at Hogwarts and reap all the benefits of being a goff."

"Wow, thanks, Brick! You're the greatest!"

"I know I am."

"G'night."

"Night, mate."

And we fell asleep. Today was the best day I'd ever had without Ebony since the day I met her.

Chapter 13.

A/N: Tara's still taking a break from writing so here I, Xanthan Gum, am, writing about some stuff. Today, I shall be writing about Brick, who in turn will be writing about a guy who writes about a guy who writes about a girl who writes her name into history by doing something unforgettable. Also, this'll end on a cliffhanger, which Tara will work around next time. Ready? Here we go! Oh yeah, I almost forgot, no preps.

XXXXXXXXXXXXXXXXXXXXXXXXXXXXXXXXGoffick_ButterXXXXXXXXXXXXXXXXXXXXXX XXXXXXXXXXXX

Well, I woke up the next morning. Nothing surprisin' at all. I was still on top, and was still naked (okay, I was wearin' a condom, but does that really count as a garment?), with The Mac directly below me. Fellow

goffz, you guessed it: nothin' surprisin' at all (preps would still be tryin' to figure this out – or would have jumped to the way wrong conclusion). No, I'm not gay, I just like bein' on top of people. It makes me feel superior, and as I woke up and yawned, I felt like a huge fuckin' winner.

Today was going to be my first day as the administrative head of Hogwarts. Hogwarts...Hogwarts. Hmm, that name seems old. It's about as old as the school, which is in itself too old to still be standing. Hm...my first official dilemma. To tear down and rebuild, or not? In the end, I decided that would be the way to go. Once the castle was rebuilt, I'd rename it, and only then would it truly be mine. So I went to my office (formerly Dumbledunce's) and called some people, who came over in the afternoon. They were just about to get started when...

"What the flyin' fuck is goin' on here?!"

Ignorin' Dumblestupid's insultin' outburst, I quickly began jottin' some stuff. I wrote about a guy who wrote about a guy who wrote about a girl that wrote her name into history by doin' somethin' unforgettable. Sounds like Ebony. *Man-Sigh.* And then the first of the huge balls known as wreckin' balls (for the benefit of prepz *(grr)*, the proper pronunciation is **reh-kin' buh-alls**) hit the Astronomy tower hard-on! No, I don't have one at the moment, but then again, I did not know until now that violent destruction makes me super-horny.

Suddenly, I heard some screamin' from the castle. I then realized I had forgotten to do somethin' important earlier. Fortunately, all the goffik peoples were already outside with me, so only the preps were still in. However, I didn't want to get the sh!t beat out of me by angry prep parents, so I signed into law an order sayin' everybody must evacuate. To cut an already short story even shorter *(sorry, preps, but this is Tara's fic, so I don't mean My Immortal or this fic, whatever it's called)*, all the preps who were meant to survive did, and some of them died. I wish they had all died (the preps, I mean). One prep, whose preppy name was Britney (in case you all forgot, she's the Gryfindor prep that keeps pissin' off Ebony with her preppiness and preppy ways), came up to me haughtily.

She looked pissed off, but I didn't like her because she wasn't built to please (if you know what I mean, *wink*). That reminds me, when it comes to girls, I find that the bigger the cushion, the sweeter the pushin'!

"What the hell?! I was in the middle of studyin' when the tower began collapsin'! I was half expectin' there to be a big explosion like at the end of the Lord of the Rings when Sauron blows up when his tower gets killed!"

"Yeah, the school needed a face-lift!"

"You suck!"

"Prep, leave now and never come back! For my next official act, I hereby expel you and all preps who will not convert to the ways of bein' goffic!"

Once that was settled, The Mac came up to me.

"Nice! What next?"

"Now I pronounce you, The Mac, as Hogwarts's newest graduate, and –
"

"Hogwarts? I thought you were going to change it to something more goffig!"

"Yeah, I'll need the co-headmistress's counsel before I do anything; on that, and that'll only be after the castle is rebuilt to look even more cool and gofficker than before!"

"Ebony?"

"Yeah, I guess that's her name."

"Cool. Well, continue."

"Right. As I was sayin', I hereby pronounce you a graduate of...this hallowed ground for goffz...and furthermore, will allow you to continue

to live here. Furthermore (and this is completely optional) *(I'm not talkin' to you readers – except for this group of words inside this set of parentheses),* if you will serve as my advisor, I can guarantee you a sufficient income of golden galleons, blood rubies, and the finest sapphires and emeralds as monthly compensation for your companionship and services rendered to me and to the school, courtesy of that prep Britney's family."

"Oh, hell yeah! But how are you goin' to get all that money from them?"

"Oh, believe me, I have a way," I said, lookin' into his eyes so that he could see into my own goffick eyes. He could not look away, but nodded.

"You're right as usual! I accept all the provisions!"

"Great, then it's settled! Would you be willin' to start now, or is later better?"

"I can start now. What do you require of me, my liege?"

"I require some knowledge, specifically, how I'm goin' to fund the rebuilding costs of the school."

"BRICK, YOU MOTERFUCKIN' DUMBASS!!! IN ONLY A SINGLE DAY, YOU'VE SINGLE-HANDEDLY RUINED THE HOGWARTS TRADITION AND EXPERIENCE FOR EVERYONE! ON TOP OF THAT, YOU DESTROYED THE CASTLE AND EXPELLED HALF THE STUDENT BODY!" DumbleRainsOnMyParade shouted to me. I didn't care though, because he's no longer the headmaster, and fuck whatever opinion he has.

"I'm reportin' this to Gordon Brown, the Prime Minister of the United Kingdom!" McGonagall said to nobody in particular (especially not to me). She turned and started to leave the area.

"Wait, my sexy and sultry girl-toy! Why not inform the Minister of Magic about this heinous act instead?"

"Because you know as well as I do that the naked bein' over there *(that's*

me, Brick!) is a terrorist."

"I'm not a fuckin' terrorist! I just get angry sometimes!" I shouted angrily.

"Brick, WTF is goin' on?" a familiar voice shouted.

I turned around, and there stood Ebony, flanked by some other goffick people! I felt happy like I do after eatin' a whole pound of fried butter and down a couple butter beers!

Chapter 14. Never Enough.

AN/: Koy, Im back, pplz. B4 I begn, I'd like 2 thonk XG 4 de last fuo chappies. U rok!11 O yah, and I ned to tell da vyoowers what ive been up 2. Well, me nad XG finally got it on on on Trusday nite, and aftur he putt on a command, he put his meatstick in2 my slit and we did it 2getheer!!!11111111111 When he left, tho, I got so sad that I went to the bathruum to cut my wrists, then red the latte st ishue of Goff Girl Weekly while I waited 4 it 2 stop bleeding.

*XXXXXXXXXXXXXXXXXXXXXXXXXXXXXXXXXXXX666XXXXXXXXXXXXXXXXXXXXXXXXXXXX
XXXXXXXXXXXXX*

1s the dust setld, we got up from da crater which was smoking b/c we had just crash-landed in a notso Sublette way. I was followed by the ppl

I had cum w/. B4 us stood the rubes of the ruins of Hogwartz. In front of that, Brick was shooting angrily at Dumbledore and McGlockenschpiel while Mr. Norris used Flounder as a masturbatory ade b/c he had no one else left 2 do it 4 him.

"Brick, WTF is gong on?/" I asked confuscious.

"Well, Enoby, I became headmaster a few days ago. I didn't want to become headmasturbater at 1st, but when Dumblefork left, I really had no choice. Besides, I've been living in secret in the office 4 2 weeks instead."

"I'm still headmaster!" Dumbledore exclaimed, but just then a boom of thunder sot out of the gray sky. I looked up at the sky, there was not a cloud in it. A gr8 wind blew past us suddenly, and then there was laughter behind us!!!11

"Nyah! I'm back!" It was...............Voldertom!1

Brick got all pissed just then, and so did I and Gahrid.

"Brick, com dwn!" I shrieked, but Brick still looked pist.

"Not now, Ebondy, I have to kill Your Mom!" Brick said.

"Wait, did you just threaten a family mmber of another student, you lowly-worms cumbag!" McGonagain shasked (itzs a fuoshun of shouterd and asked).

"We don't have time 4 this!1 This is a disaster zone hyah! Sum1 must make a sacrifice 2 save us!" Dumbledore shouted as he took leadership.

"No, stupid! I'm the headmaster, and I call the shots, and Your Mom MUST DIES!!!!!!!!!!" Brick screamed in such a goffikx voick that I nearly wanted to cry tears of blood onto Gerard's shirt b/c it was such a byutiful speach. However, Gerard was still wearing only his manties so I hard to cry on Hagrid's shirt.

"OMFG, ENOBY, WHY YOU DO THAT?" he shouted to the sky also crying tearz of bluud. Draco came out and started crying two.

Volzeimormon got mad then and made a speech that was very long and made me want to slit my wrists, (which eye deed) and it took until it stopped bleeding for him to finally shut up. *(A/N; Kay, Im aboot 2 try 2 right a long partagrampa, so try not 2 fall aspeel, kay?")*

"OMFG, u stupid pplz! Thou alt make me want to slit my wrists and give a speech so long that I have to keep on speaking until it stops bleeding!!!1 I need 2 adres each of thou individually so that thou wilt all know all thine fates! Fustly, Ebony Dark'ness Dementia Raven Way. Thou art my rival, and I shalt kill thou before the end, as well as all thine friends. There's nothing thou can doeth to stopeth meth. Next, I mustard salad addressing Brickbuilder Robert Zanganese Portuguese Siamese Lebanese Chinese Japanese Cantonese Thollerson. Thoueth mighteth bieth theyeth headmastereth ofeth Hogwartzeth, buteth thoueth arenoteth powerfuleth enougheth toeth challengeth meth. Bark Bark said the coat. MUCH HARPOON ATTACHED!!11 Thou wilt knoweth my coming when thou seeth much of flying away the snake danubing from the Dark Market!!!11 Now thou, Dumblebore. I hath much hatred for thou. Betwixt thou and I, thou art too old to be ye headmaster anymore! And I hate thou!11 As for thou, Minerva McGonagallon, I must say I never liked thou, but good job on turning the old man to the light! Captain, we're taking on water! Now, I shalt address thou, Gerard Way. Thou art a fucking mortal, but thou hast the power to make stupid-smart goff girls fall for you. I want 2 kill thou, but at the same time, I feel like I'm young and horny again, and I start to see Y they fall for u lyk yu doo. Still, I h8 goffick people, cause I want them 2 dye, and I want them two die b/c I hate them! Sid, why the fuck did you pour salt into your sock drawer? I could've gone outside to smoke a chimichanga or two, u motherfucking son of a bitch!!!111 Now its thine turn, Draco...........................Will u tech me to becum like the old motherfucker (Im talcum powdering about Dublecheeseburger) was? I want 2 know what it's like on da other syde!!1 And Hogridmapper, you

should just give up on the goff immature tastyfan, b/c u R 2 old. Finally u, Britney. I don't mean 2 sound like a kweer or anything, but I think unicorns and reignboze R awsum!!!!111 Thyou aret my daughter, and I am your daddy! Who's your daddy? I'm your daddy! Come. Come to me. Yes, come to me. Come. Cum. Sweetie, come to daddy! Come. Get your sweet little ass over here and give your father a hug! Don't make me beg now! Get over here! Come! COME! CONE! CUM ONTO ME ALL FUCKING READY!!!!!!!!!11111111111111111" Did you know that treez have heart attacks???????///

"I've had enuff of this!" Dumblemoore proclaimed, stepping up to a podium that appeared out the ground like as though it had been raised out of the ground magically!! "Leave Britney alone!"

"No" all the goffick people

"I want it so bad!" Britney and Satan orgasmed in perfect unison.

"Wait, where's Brick?" Vampier sketched as he came to us.

"Hiya!" Brick hiyaed, doing a really cool goff-ninja kick and knocking Voldertaic out. Standing up, he said something in a voice that = his action.

"I let you live...4 now..."

I got hot all over looking at Brick, he looked exactly lyk Capt. Orgazmo from the really cool cult film Orgazmo.

"Mew! Mew, mew!" He shooted at Britney and Volzeboss an imaginary orgazmoradar that caused them to blast off *(lyk in the anime)* while making a wet in their paunts. They would now oh us jewels and gold and all that good stuff. Dontchu fink CNN reports good newz?

With that, the sun had set completely, and court was dismissed until more evidence could be collected to analyze the next day.

"Hey, Ebony, wannat come see a GC concert with me and Draco?"

Vampire asked.

"Sure!" i said nonchalantly.

"I guess I will cum 2" Brick supplemented.

"Gr8, then itz a d8!"

*XXXXXXXXXXXXXXXXXXXXXXXXXXXXXXXXXX666XXXXXXXXXXXXXXXXXXXXXXXXX
XXXXXXXXXXXXX*

That evening, we went 2 tha concert as planned. Gerard had to leave earlier so he could get with his band to prepare 42nite. We all rode in Draco's car, which we had tamed from the wild after it got lost in the forbidden forest and we coodnt find it for 3 days grace (getit, cause they're goffick?). Oh yah, 3DG would also be playing at the concert 2nite.

We did drugs and heroine on the way to the concert. We got all funny then. Brick tried to pick his ears with his toes, Draco and Vampire tried nasal sex, and I wanted 2 C what wood happen if I put some of the E in my you-know-what. We made it to the concert safely, but the ride was so much fun.

Unless they're all young ppl, how are these people we show on this screen? The young generation, that sick generation... *(A/N: Sry, im litening 2 Rob Zombie, hu is a goffick ghoust)* No, he's not in the concert, stupid! Y wuud u fink dat?

MCR was up first, singing their song 'Helena'. It was so fucking butifel. Gerard even winked me be4 he got of stage.

Ate that thyme, I began to hear sum pepl shouting!11 It was Draco, Vampire, and Brick all having a freeway fight.

"I asked her first, so im here date!"

"Yeah, bt we came here in mah car!"

"That I stole the keys 2!"

"u mothefucka!1'

"your granma21!"

"OMFG, EBONY, I WANNA SEX U UP!!!1'"

"........."

"...butter..."

"...........goffick pizza............"

"What the foking hell R u doing here, Hargrate?" iAsked.

"I HORNY, SO ME COME TWO GOFFICK CONCERT 2 CE IF U IN DA MOOD! IF U NOT, THAT COOL. ME JUST WAIT TILL YOU GET MOOD AND WE CAN SEX!"

"Are yu fucking insane?!" I shouted angrily. "Of course not I'm in the mood! Youre a fucking adult!11"

"I saw Eboby first, perps!" Brick cheered.

"Who you calling a prep, prep?" Drace then added.

"N'body" called Vampire, and they all jumped onto each other!1 *(no not in that way u pervs)*. They began to fight and beat up each other!

"Can u guyz plz stop fiting, 3DG is about to play!" I screamed.

A feud minutes l8er, the 3DG guys started to play. The were all wering baggy black polyester cargo pants with gofk silver metal chains coming out of the pockets, black tshirts that said #DG on them, and sum black shoes. I couldnt tell if they were wearing black socks.

"*So what if you can see the darkest side of me, no one will ever change this animal I have become*" Joel Madden sang ectopically. I started making out with Vampire.

"Ebony, Im mad at u!" Brick shouted, and he punched Vampire so hard that he fell over splitting blood from his nose holes.

"OMG, Brick!" I freaked out.

"O grow a pear, Enoby!" Brick shouted. He turned and ran into security pplz!1

"Where do u fink youre going?" one of them asked.

"The fuck ud like to know!" Brick said, fighting them as if they were Your Mom (A/N: That's Brick's name for Volizmort)

"Hes resisting!"

"Sir, ur under a rest! U have the rite to shut the fuck up!" (A/N: su du yu, prepz!)

"I beg to differential" Brick said, melting the handcuffs with his goffick yellow eyes. "I want you too ded!" and he killed the guards also with his eyes!!!1

"**OMFG, BRICK'S A TERRORIST!!!11**" Hairgrid shooted.

"How many times do I have to tell you stoopid ppl?!1 Im not a fuckin' extortionist!!1"

Just then, Volzemort appeared!

"I never left u no" he said in a vane effort 2 brake the 666th (getdit, cause I'm a satanista) wall. "I have a secret to tell thou alt! Brick's a moogle!oneone"

Everybuddy glared at Brick angrily because we were angry to find out that he was not magic!!1

XXXXXXXXXXXXXXXXXXXXXXXXXXXXXXXXXXXXX666XXXXXXXXXXXXXXXXXXXXXXXXX
XXXXXXXXXXXXX

A/N: No, everyting fine w/ moi & Xanthan Gum. Its part of the plort, prepz!!1
Join me nxt time when I pst da new chpter!!

Chapter 15.

AN: OK, I wonder whatitll take 2 get u prepz 2 sshut de FUCk up and sotp
flaming teh story! Im so sick of u, it makes me wunt 2 kill you all!!!1Fangz to
mah horny for prooping dis (geddit? Satan!1).

XXXXXXXXXXXXXXXXXXXXXXXXXXXXXXXXXXXXX666XXXXXXXXXXXXXXXXXXXXXXXXX
XXXXXXXXXXXXX

I didn't want to bleeve what I had herd. I prayed to g-o-d (I'm Satanist,
so im not saying that goddang wurd) that it was all a lie. Sanddunes

later, I began running towards the exit.

"Ebony, Ebnoy, wherefore art thou going?" Volzemort asked.

"Of fuck off, u fucking prep!" I shouted back angrily.

"Wait!" he shouted lightly, but I kept storming off.

"Wait!" all my friends called, but I keept walking out.

"Wait! Bri"ck shouted but he was the center of all my hatred now.

"Wait!" shouted the teachers from the skuol, but I was 2 mad to care rite now.

"Wait?" stated some preps who came to tha concert to learn 2 b goffick but coodnt because they didnt no whut goffick is. I put up all my middle fingers at them.

"Waitr!" Voldemort called to me again, and only this time did I lissen to what he has to say. "Wut if I toold u there was another way?"

"What, u mean u cloned me and Gerard's baby into 1 whole bing?" I asked sarcasmically.

"No" he snarkled. "I'm talking about you coming aweigh with me for a wile!"

Now I was interested. I wanted to here more. But something didn't make much sense.

"Something doesn't add up1!" I shrieked. "Yuo aren't planning to.........kill me, are you?"

I saw Vozlemorte taking out a goffick black banana thing than hastility putting it in his pants. I didn't know what it was. We began walking to his car, a black and orange lamborgenie. Volzemorte was vvearing some gray robes, grey potatosack shoes, and no nose. I looked quickly into his face. He had no nose still and some sorrowful red-orange eyes, which is

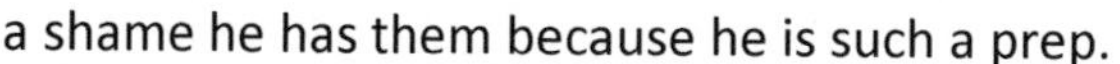

a shame he has them because he is such a prep.

I was going with him because he had offered me a release, and I was going to take him up on it!!111

Chapter 16.

A\N: I don't kare abot wut prpez think. STOP FLAMING TEH FOKING STOREE!!!1 Fangz to XG for maeking dis chapy magic! Goffic frenches!!1

XXXXXXXXXXXXXXXXXXXXXXXXXXXXXXXXXXXXX666XXXXXXXXXXXXXXXXXXXXXXX XXXXXXXXXXXX

"HUNNEE, we're hohm!" Voldemort sang lovelily as we walked in thru the front door. I didn't know who he was talking about.

"OMFG, you have a GF?!" I demented.

"Not really, I used to have a wife by the name of Purple the Pill." he danced.

I gaspt. "OMG, you had importance?"

"NOOOO!!"

Just then, Britney came down. She waz wearing white leather shoes with no socks, a flannel skut so short I kood see her hot pnk PNTEES!, a plain white tshert, and a red and blue tie. I fuckin h8 dat little bitch! I ran up to her to tackle her (no, I don't like her!!1)

"Help me!" she squeaked in that irritating voice of hers. Then she grabbed my shirt and ripped it off!!1 You could only see my black leather bra on my Clearasil back.

"Youre going 2 pay 4 that!" Ice creamed. (an I love screaming for goffik black ice cream!!!)

Suddenly, we became aware that someone was watching us...

TBC, ppl!

Chapter 17.

A/N: What the fucking hell, prepz?! Tara is real! If she wasn't, then why would I, Xanthan Gum, still be giving it to her? Huh? You preps are unbelievable. And "fellow goff", you're just a fucking poser prep! How dare you call yourself one of the honorable goffz! We're a respectable culture, and I won't hear of you taking a shit on it!

XXXXXXXXXXXXXXXXXXXXXXXXXXXXXXXXXXXGoffik_ButterXXXXXXXXXXXXXXXXXX XXXXXXXXXXXXX

I was fuckin' pissed. Ebony had called me a prep! That fuckin' bitch *(A/N: Tara, I love you!!!)*!

I walked down some street, munchin' on the one consolation I still had: butter. Turnin' the corner, some preps pointed at me and started laughin'. I was gettin' even more pissed by them, so I fuckin' killed them. Then I felt a little better cause they wouldn't laugh at me anymore. Then I kuntinued *(get it? Prepz, don't answer)* to walk. I finished eatin' the butter I had. Then I remembered I still had to fuckin' rule the motherfuckin' school, so I went back and did some stuff that would work out to the benefit of **TRUE** goffz *(A/N: Posers suck!)*.

THE END

A Vampre Wil Nevr Hurt You

Chapter 1.

(AN- ok gyz dis iz da real tara ok! An if u say dat its not da real tara den ur a prep! So me an 1 of muh frendz, her namez haly, we decidd 2 mak a nu fanfic! So den I askd raven 2 help me wit da spellin an stuff. Fangz raven and hayly! U gyz both rok!!!!!!!!! 11111111)

Hi my name is Luna Lovegood. At least that's what my mother fucking

parents called me. Now you can call me Moon Shad'ow Ivory Tearz Florin. Actually my mom was ok but then she killed herself when I was nine. If that wasn't bad enough my dad would make me do all the housework and if I didn't then he would beat me and rape me. So today I decided to run away to my friend Cho's house in Tokyo. Actually Cho changed her name about the same time I changed mine. Now she's Eztli Kyoko. Eztli means blood, she chose it cause she is goffik *(AN- I spelled that right preps ok!)* like me. When we decided to be goffik we died *(get it, cause I'm goffik)* our hair. Mine is now long and black with red blue and purple streaks in it. Eztli's hair was already black since she's from Japan so she just put red streaks in it with blue tips. We also dress goffikly, for example today I was wearing a black sleeveless top that had lacey corset stuff on the front and it showed off my boobs. I was also wearing a black miniskirt with lace on the ends. I had black fishnet tights and I was wearing goffik black armbands. I had tall black lace up boots on too. Eztli was wearing a long sleeved top with corset stuff on the front and its sleeves were all droopy at the ends. She also had a really tight and short mini skirt with chains on it and it there was lace all over the bottom. Her shoes were plaid and they had really big platforms.

So today we were going back to Hogwarts on the train. When we got on the train a bunch of preps stared at us. We stuck out middle fingers up at them and they got scared and ran away. Me and Eztli found a compartment where out friends B'loody Mary Smith (who was Hermione), Dark'nd Heart (who was Jenny), and Gianna Virginia Wyatt Diamond *(that's you hayley you rock girl!)* were all shitting together, they were wearing all goffik clothes from hot topic like corsets and suspenders and big black trench coats .

"Hey," we all said depressed.

"Oh my fucking Satan, guess why me and Eztli came to the train together!" I almost shouted. So then I told them all about how I ran away from my dad.

"What a fucking bustard!" B'loody Mary shouted angrily. Everyone else

agreed.

Then someone came. It
was..
Draco Malfoy!

(AN- fangz (get it) 4 reedin muh story gyz! an im guna b on vcation 4 al of nxt week so only haly cn updat! plz reviow, but ony gud 1s!!!!!!111111111111)

Chapter 2

AN: Ok this is Haylys chapter now me n tara take it in turds hop u liek it xoxoxoxoxo luff yew gurl!

I started at my painted black and pink nailz as Draco came.I couldnt look at him not after what had happuned between us last year so I just started pulling at my clothes, A black long sleved tshirt with pink skullz on it and a black miniskit with pink converse, I was wearing a bit of eyeliner with some clear lipgolls and foundation, My blonde hare was

strate nd down to my waste.

He sat next to me and opposhite Moon Hi he sed shyly hi i bumbled back I cant beleve that it was only last skull year he was kising me goodbi and teeling me he naevar wntd 2 see me agen. I WANTED TO FUKIN PUNCH THAT MOTHAFUKKERS FACE OPEN!1. He had hurt me so much dat I nerly tried 2 kill myself, he broke my fart.

It was quiet sudenly moon sed why r u being quit 2 me Darco looped up i told her i had a hedache and she began talking 2 B'loody Mary about MCR' Gerard is so fukin hoot i herd moon say I cunt take it no more. I ran 2 da toilets in tears, Darco Followd me

I looked myself in the cubickle and began to silt my rists the blood felt so good i was realy upset. Gianna Darco called Piss oof i dnot want 2 talk to you! i schemed back:

Gianna if u dnt cum out and talk to me then i'll have to cum in. he resnorted Draco just leave me alone i sed crying sullenly he appeared in front of me, Gianna im so sorry he said, i never meant to burt you, I love you he sed I believed himn

ok but wat ur gonna do about it i sed

he cleaned in and kisd me his died blak hare touched my face

this is wat im gunna do about it he sed

I kissed him back, suddenly he gut on top of me and started to unlace my corset i took off his top and tite genes He started kissing my neck sexually den we had sex and we had sex 4 da frisk time in 4 month, I holed noisily and began to scream ah! Ah! Ah! I smiled, I saw a load of Ravenhoars in da halway and told them to fuk oof

Den he got oof me zippsed his troosers and wanked away

Draco WTF!?? i cried angstily flowing him

He paused, cum on he sed

Okai I followed him bak 2 da compartmejt.

Chapter 3.

(AN- ok y rnt me an hayly getin ne revoiws,??? srsly hyz if u red it den u hav 2 revoiw, ok now dats a nu rul!!!!!!!!! an fangz agen 2 raven 4 helpin me wif da story an spellin and fangz 2 haly 4 makin a gr8 2nd chapta u gyz boff rok!!!!!!!!!!!!!!!!!!!111111111111111111111111)

Whenever Giana and Drako came back into the train room me and

B'loody Mary were still talking about MCR and how sexy Gerard Way was. When Gianna came in then she sat down and looked kind of mad. Draco tried to sit down next to her but she looked really evil at him and you could tell he thought it was hot but then she told him to leave.

"Fine well then can Moon come out here for a minute???"

"Just give us a minute to talk and then shell come out, k." Then he left.

"He kissed me!!!!!!" Gianna roared.

"But I thought that you liked him so why are you so mad then."

"I never told you guys but at the end of last year he told me I was a stupid preppy bitch who should be in Hufflepuff and then he said he never wanted to see me again. So I dont know what hes trying to do this time but I dont think I should get back together with him."

None of us knew what to say about that so we just stared at Gianna for a minute but we all knew what a bastard Draco was being then Dark'nd Heart reminded me that Draco was waiting to talk to me so I left the train compartment and went into the hall.

"What to you want, bastard?" I yelled.

"Come here." And then he took me to a different room that had no one in it then he started to kiss me. "What the hell!!!!" I shouted. But he didnt listen he just did a spell that made me keep quiet. He took off my top and even my bra but then when he started to take off my mini skirt I kicked him in the boy thingy. Then I made him undo the spell so I could talk again and I put on all my clothes and went back to my own room.

"What did he want" everyone asked me when I got there.

"I dont want to talk about that bastard right now, k!!!" They didnt ask again.

Then it was time to get off the train and go to dinner. After we ate we

went to our Slytherin room and went to bed. Me, Gianna, Eztli, Dark'nd Heart, and B'loody Mary were all in the same bedroom together. (Except we werent in the same bed you sicko) After they were all asleep I was still awake thinking about what happened with Draco on the train. Then I heard someone open the door.

"Whos there!!!" I whispered cause I didnt want to wake up my friends. It was Draco! He did the same spell that made me not make noise, and he climbed on top of me and started taking off my clothes and kissing me. He was already naked so he put his boys thingy in my girls thingy and we did it together. He was really hot and he looked a lot like Gerard Way so I was really starting to enjoy this. Then someone yelled "MOON AND DRACO WHAT THE FUCK ARE YOU DOING!!!!!!!!!!!"

It was Gianna!

"I'm soory! Draco started it, not me!" I yelled.

"Well Gianna my dad says I cant have a girlfriend since Im going to work for Voldymurt so thats why I had to break up with you but since Im backat school now I wanted to get back together! But then when I came in your train room I saw how buaetiful Moon is and I wanted to be with her now..."

Giannna looked seriously mad right now..........................

(AN- ok gyz now im back frum my vaction so i can updat a lot mor but only if i git revoiwews!!!!!!!!!!!!!!!!!!111111111111111)

Chapter 4.

AN/ okai its hayly agen, tara ur chapat cocked so hard it was kul u rok girlie!1

I wanted to kil dat bastard!1

I ran cryin 2 da bathtomb *(geddit?)*were I cryd, I cryd so mch dat my eyeliner ran doom my face. Den…. Draco walked in!1

Im sory he sed

FUK OF LOODER! I sed I ran out da roon cryin, I put oan sum moar iliner and a black prom-stile dress wif blk high I came out da room.

I ran out of da Slytherin vommon room suddenly I gut 2 da grate hal.

I collapsed.

Wen I was conscientious again I luked up and saw 2 bois, DEY WER FRUM FUKIN GRIFFYNDOR!

It wuz......Harry Potter ands Ron Weasley

R u ok sed harry

Yeh I sed

Just den Dumbledor and Moon came in da corridor Darco was following dem

Fuk of Darco I sed

Harry and Ron luked shoked.

I gut up and wlked away

Harry and Ron flowed me

Cum wif us dey sed.

Dey tuk me 2 dumbelhores office

Processor dumblehore dey sed can Gianna cum in2 griffindor

Letz c wat da sorting hat sez he sed

He tuk da hat dune and placd it on ma hud like he had dun in yr1

DA HAT SED I SHULD HAV BEN IN GRIFINDOR ANYWAY CUZ I WASN'T EVIL11

We all gapsed

Suddenly Moon, etzreli, b'loody maru and Draco came

Chapter 5.

(AN- ok now dis iz taras chapta agen hayly ur chapta waz awsum!1 fangz 4 makin anudr gr8 1!!!1111 an aso fangz 2 raven 4 da spelin agen u rok gurl!11 o an fangz 4 finly revioewin da story but cud u plz mak dem gud revieows????)

Me, Eztli, B'loody Mary, and Drako came in Dumblydore's orifice. Gianna, and those two stupid Gryffindor prepz were in there to and

Giana had the sorting hat on her head.

"Hey guys whats going on here" Eztli said.

Giana started to cry and said "THE SORTING HAT SAYS I SHOULD BE IN GRYFFINDOR!!!11111"

"But Giana, that would mean your a prep! WHAT THE FUCK IS GOING ON HERE!" I roared.

Dumbledore just handed her some Gryffindor clothes. Me and all the Slytherins walked out of the office and into the Slytherin living room. I was really confused cause Gianna was my friend but she was also a prep since she was in Gryffindor. I decided I need to talk to her so I ran out of the door and I wore my invisilinblity coat, I followed some preppy doosh that was in Gryffindor and she looked like Hilary Duf *(AN I fokin h8 dat lil slut!1)* to the Gryffindor room. I ran up the stairs to where Giannas new rom was. I opened the door and................. she was having sexx with Harry and Ron was holding a camera!!!111

"You fucking hore!111" I screamed at her. Then I ran away.

The next day, we were in class Giana came up to me and said "Harry is my bf now so you can have Draco. And Im not dressed like a prep so you can tell I didn't want to be in Gryffindor."

I decided I was going to forgive her so then I went to tell Draco the good news.

(AN- ok I hav a feelin da tid siz guna b a rly gud chaptr so revieow it plz an fangz!)

Chapter 6.

(AN: Ok guise dis is Hayly Tara u rok & fankuu 4 da god revues,ur awsum)

I cryd in da room, Hairy & Ron wos nice but dey wuz prepz!1111

I thort for a bit Sullenly I had an idea!11

I flet around in muh pocket 4 my wand, I grabbed it and pulld.

Ok guise I sed ur getting a makeover

"GOFFIKUS!" I schemed

DEY WAS HANDSUM!

Harry wus wearing black sk8r pants and a blak Blink 183 Tshit and Ron wus wearing A red entinies top and tite emo jeans. Dey both had loads of eyeliner on AND DEY LOOKED OF FUKKIN HAWTT!!!1111111

I fort of Draco

I ran oout cring

I ran 2 da forbidden forest

I shat under a tree, it had been reigning so I new id get muh Blak nee-hi boots and muh purpill skit wet and durty.

I cryd so hard I swore my eyeballs would cum out I had eyeliner al down ma face, suddenly Draco came there.

WHY DID U CUM!1111 I SHOTTED AIRGRILLY

I wanted to c if u wer okai he sed

WELL IM FINE I SED

U DNT LOOK IT! HE RESNORTED BAK

FUK OF FUK OF! I showted

I RAN UP 2 HIM AND STARTED TITTING HIM U BASTRAD!!1111111111111111111111 I screeemed at him He began to bleed as I punched nd kikd him!

Den Moon came!

GIANNA WTF!?!?!?!?!?!?!?!??!!?1/1/1/1/1/1/1/1/1/1 she sed

I HATE HIM MOON, HES A FARTBREAKER HELL DO DA SAM 2 U!11 I SED

Den I ran away leeving Darco blooding in da foreset.

I ran in2 Hairy in skull I hugged him den cried

I LOV U! I sed

I lov u 2 he sed but wats da matter

Dracos a motherfucking bastard I sed

Well I no dat sed harry

Den I had 2 go c profezzor McGonagoogle abut sum Transfiguration werk I had to do (CUZ I WAS DED GOOD AT TIT!11)

Welcum Gianna she sed

Hello Profezzor I sed

I'm plezzed 2 hav u in my hoes

Thank u I sed

Nao herez da spels 4 u

I saw Draco and Moon ootsid da skool dey wer with

VOLDYMURT AND
BELLATRICKS!111
11
11
11
11

(DATS HOW SHOKED I WUS LULZ)

Chapter 7.

(AN- hayly ur chaptrt waz so gr8!!!!11111 an fangz 2 ravn 4 da spelin help agen. O an sum retardd prepy dush bag told me I waz a pozer in da reviewz I meen srsly wtf. But oderwiz fangz 4 da gud 1s)

Me draco voldemurt and belatrix lestrang were al walking outside. Suddenly Giana came running outside too.

"MOON WHAT ARE YOU ARE DOING WITH THE BARK LORD AND

BELLATRIX CUZ SHE'S A DEATH DEALER!!!!" Gianna screamed as she ran towards me.

"STFU, they're my friends too!" I yelled back at her.

Giana stopped yelling and said. "But what if they kill you and Draco???"

"They won't cuz we're evil to. And whenever we were talking we said that maybe the sorting hat was wrong and you should go back in Slytherin." I explained.

"But what about Harry and Ron? There my frends to."

"Didn't you do a spell on them that made them goffik? That makes them evil to. Did you notice if they worship Stan or not?"

"They do. OMFG MOON. Your so smart. No wonder all the hot goffik guys wanna have sex with you!!!!111"

That made me really happy, even though I didn't like to brag about how pretty I was. I hugged Gianna. "You know they like you too. I said.

So then Voldemurt and Bellatricks got there black mcr brooms and flu off on them. Gianna went up too the skull *(geddit cuz im goffik)* and I started to follow her but then Draco took my hand and started pulling me to Hairgrid's house.

"Draco what the fuck are you doing!!!!111" I said angrily.

He went into Hairgrid's house and closed the door. "Hagrid isn't here rite now. I think hes looking for the giants agen."

"Stupid prep. I hope they kill him to death. Wait, why are we even here."

"Cuz I have to tell you something. Ebony... I'm a vampire."

I gasped.

(AN- ok if u reed it den u hav 2 revoiw it an no meen revoiwes ok! An prepz shudnt b reedin da story newayz so juzz go fok urselvz!!!!1111 mcr and gc rok!11)

Chapter 8.

(AN: OK I WONT SUM REVEWS!1111 UR ALL REVEWING N TRAS CHAPTRS N NIT MYN!1111 REVIOW OR I WIL RITE NO MOAR! Tara ur chapat was awsum gurl!)

I wnet bak 2 skul 2 get Hary and Ron

ITZ OKAI I SED TO DEM VOLDYMURT DUS NUT WNT 2 KIL U ANYMOAR!

Harry looked at me

U MUST CUM! I shouted Pulling his red GC top angstily

Dey both came.

We waslked in2 da grounds den saw Voldymurt and Bellatricks

Hi I sed

Hi dey said back

We shall kill Dumbledore! Sed Voldmort

Yes my lord sed bellatrix

I was shocked wen Harry agred

Den I saw moon and Draco cum out Hairgrids cabin

Dmbelldhor walkd out of skool

'ABRA KEBABRA!' We all shooted da spell with our wands

DUMBLEDOR WAS DED

Profezzor McGonagoogle and Profezzor snp screemed

We al ran away to Darcos hoes

WE COULDN'T GO BAK 2 HOGWITS!

Wen we gut dere me an moon put on sum eyeliner foundation and lipshtick. She put on a blak corset and a purple skirt wif blak kne high bots, she luked amazing. I crueled muh pink hair and put on a red lace dress wif pointy blak high heels.

I cryd and slit muh rists, everyone came and askd igf I wuz ok

Yuh im ok fangz I sed mopping up da blud.

We went in2 da frunt rume

Dere was a nock at da door

It was.......Mad eye muddy!

HE HAD CUM 2 PUT US IN ASSKABIN!1

Chapter 9.

(AN- dis iz tara agen. ok gyz now it iznt fare dat I git al da revieowz and hayly hadly getz n e so rember 2 revioew her chaptrz 2!!!!!!!!1111 and haly ur chaapter wuz awsum!!1 o, and sum1 sed dat they wantd darco 2 beet up mudy an I thot dat waz kin ov funy so im guna do dat, lolz. If u reed den u hav 2 revew an ony gud 1s!!!!11 o an fangz (geddit, cuz im goffik) 2 raven 4 helpin me wif da spellin!!!111 stup flamin muh story prepz!!!!!!1111111)

When Mad I Moody came into the house Draco was really mad. "What the fuck are you doing here!!!" he shouted sexily.

"I'm taking you to Akzaban cuz you killed Dumblydork." He explained.

"NO YOU ARENT!!!!!!!!" Draco screamed at him. Then he started hitting Moddy and punching him. Then he bit Moody on the neck and drank all of his blood so Moody was dead now. Everyone cheered.

"OMFG, Draco! Are you a vampire??? Cuz you drank Moody's blood!" said Gianna.

"Yeah. I guess its not a secret anymore!" said Draco shyly.

"Hey Draco. You should give me a tour of your house!" I said excitedly. So then he took me around his house and showed me everything while Voldymurt, Bellatricx, and Gianna waited. Then he took me to his room

"Moon, I really love you and I want to have sex with you so can we have sex?" he asked me. I really wanted to have sex with him too so I started taking all of my clothes off and so did he and then we got on his bed. We started to kiss passively and then he put his really big glock in my girl's thingy and we did it together.

"OH OH OH OH OH!" I shouted cuz I was getting an orgasm. I didn't even care if the other people in the house heard.

Finally we fell asleep together. Wheneever we woke up we said, "I love you" to each other and then we put our clothes on. I was wearing a red plaid mini skirt that had ruffly stuff on the bottom and black fishnets. I had a black lace up corset with red roses on it. I was wearing black lace up platform boots. I put on my white foundation even though I was already pale and tons of black eyeliner. Draco was wearing baggy black pants with chains on them and a black MCR (arnt dey so awsum!!!) tshirt. He was also wearing white foundation and lots and lots of balck eyeliner. He looked so sexy that I wanted to have sex with him again but I didn't cuz we had to go downstairs cuz the rest were probably

wondering were we were.

Whenever we walked downstairs, Harry and Ron were there! Only they weren't dressed like preps cuz Gianna had done a spell on them to make them goffik.

"OMFG, what the fuck are you doing here!!!" I said.

(AN- omfg dis story iz rly fun 2 rite so dats y me an haly hav a lot of cahptrz evry day. Remmbr 2 revoew halyz chaptre cuz I fink deyre awsum!!!11 u rok gurl!!11)

Chapter 10.

We wer al reeding da daily prophet wen we saw a sign da sed MCR & GC wil hav a concert!

We al gosped, dat nite, Moon, Me, Dracdo, Harry and Ron went 2 c them play, I couldc moon droling ova Gererd Way, closse ur mpth! I sad Lol she sed bak, After we gut bak frm da concert we decidd we had 2 go bak 2 hogwerts.

Wen we gut dere I saw a sine dat sed: WANTED: MOON,GIANNA, DRACO, HARRY AND RON- DER IS A REWARD BCOZ DEY KILD DUMBELHOR.

I began 2 cry, Hairy put his arm around me.

It's okay he sed wit his sexy voice

Sullenly he puld da invincibility cloke over us and we went 2 da lake!

Den we had sex 3 tims in a roe,

He was ded gud

Sudeently I gospd

IT WAS PROFEZZOR MCGOOGLE!

Chapter 11.

(AN- fangz 4 finaly revoiwung haly's chaptrs gyz!!!!! An alsso sum1 els sed dat im nut da rel tara WTF!!!!!!! I mean I cn sho u my fb an stuf srsly pm me azkin me an I wil giv u da link. Odderwiz fangz 4 da gud 1z also speshul fangz 2 raven 4 da help u rok guirl!!!!! And u do 2 hayly!)

I saw Mcgoongal walking by the lake. I think that's were Giana and Hary

went. But they had the invincibility clock so they will be ok if they don't say anything.

Suddenly snape came up behind me Draco, Vlodemort, and Bellatricx. Belltrix screamed and ran away and Voledmurt ran after yeliing "STOP I LOVE YOU!"

"Avabra Kevadra!" I said as I pointed my wond sexily at Snap.

Then McGanggale came running from the lake and Draco and Gianna wjere chasing her and they had there wombs pointed at her and they wre yelling spells at her and then I heard Gianna say "Abra Kadavara!" and then Mcgangooogle fell over and she was dead.

"Come one guys we need to get away from here" Draco said. So then we went into the forest and we made a camp there. Gianna made sum tents apper so we went under them2 sleep. Gianna and Harry was in one, and me and draco was in a different one. I was wearing really sexy pajamas. I was wearing pink and black skull shorts that were really really short and showed off my sexy legs. Draco was staring at them but I pretended nut too notice. For my top I had on a black fishnet tube top that was really low cut so you could see all my cleavage. Draco was staring at that to.

"Hey Draco" I said seductivley. Then we started frenching each other passiontly and he took off my clothes and I took off his and we did it for the second time.

After we were done then I asked him if vampires lived forever and he said yes so then I asked how someone was made a vampire. He said that you could either be bom one or if you were bitten by a vampire then you would be one too. I asked if he would bite me so I could be a vampire too. He said ok and then he bit me. I was asleep for a long time, and then when I woke up I found Ron.

"Hi Ron" I said sexily. He said hi back.

I put my mouth on his neck like I was going to kiss him but instead I bit him too. Then I drank all his blood so he would be dead.

"Moon, what the fuck! I know your a vampire but Ron was my friend!" said Harry.

"Im sorry harry. I'll try not to kill anyone we know from now on." I said sadly.

"Well its ok he wasn't very smart anyways." Said harry.

Then…………… Eztli came! "What are you doing here!" we all said.

"Well all the goff and punk kids rebelled against the teachers and all the teachers who werent goffik we killed them. So you guys can come back to Hogwarts now." Eztli said.

Chapter 12. The Aplogee 11

(A/N Okay I think this is the final chapter now- Hayley)

I was sitting in my tent crying (after all, I was a self insert, as per with these shitty fanfics) What had Tara and Myself done? Well I could answer that

logically, we had participated in a horrifying case of cannon rape, MCR references, 'Goffik' fetish clothing and above all we had become the epitome of Mary sue.

'CANNONUS' I cried.

At that point everything changed, Teachers appeared back in their respective classrooms and Harry, Ron, Hermione, Luna and Draco were back in their common rooms. The set of Harry potter was buzzing, the filming of 'Harry Potter and the Deathly Hallows' was well underway.

That's when I realized I wasn't sitting in a tent with Harry Potter and Draco Malfoy any more. I was, of course, at home, in front of my computer mercilessly raping one of the best book series and film franchises of all time alongside a girl who is claiming to be uber-retard (or internet genius) Tara Gilesbie. I looked back over the previous chapters and was appalled by what I had written. Innuendos, intentional spelling mistakes, stupid names for cannon characters that would only ever appear once in the story and disturbing sexual relations which had been played out by the mind of 'Tara Gilesbie' littered the pages. I felt sick, then I instantly felt sorry for JK Rowling, Daniel Radcliffe and Tom Felton. There was no explanation as to why we did this, other than that we had too much time on our hands and that I finally wanted to taste the satirical value that writing a shitty parody of a fan fiction gives you, I wanted a chance to feel all that and more, but more than anything though, I wanted to work with Tara Gilesbie. Ashamed was an understatement. That's when I became enlightened, I realized that I had nothing to BE ashamed of. 'Why?' You may ask, I will tell you why. Because this is an example of the content of 90% of this website.

Appalling spelling and thesaurus overuse is rife here, as well as Mary sues and lackluster plotlines, some so loose that they could barely be described as plotlines at all, just a mass of jumbled concepts and ideas strung together with cannon rape and horrific fantasies of horny teenage girls. Then the same people who write this kind of fanfic had the audacity to come on and slag off Tara Gilesbies 'My Immortal.' Hypocrisy barely describes it. I dread to think what J.K

Rowling would think if she came on here and discovered that people are brutally butchering her stories then stitching them up again to suit their sick fantasies, come to think of it I also dread to think what Daniel Radcliffe, Rupert Grint, Emma Watson and Tom Felton (because lets face it, they are who your thinking of via visual representation when you write these piles of HP fanfiction horse shit) would think of these dreadful amateur attempts at 'literature' made by folk on here. I for one do not think chopping up and murdering JK Rowlings world is either appropriate or respectful to the woman who created this. And I do realize that it isn't just Harry Potter you all seem so intent on destroying, It's Twilight, Nightmare before Christmas, Camp Rock (although that WAS shit in the first place) and practically any other film with a 'cult. (I hate using that word but I will) fanbase. Do you really think the authors appreciate your Sues' running riot in their worlds?

After I wrote and analyzed all this, I made a cup of tea and posted chapter 12. Aptly named 'The Apology.'

Chapter 13.

Yes. This is "Tara's" chapter again.

Did you notice those little quotation marks around Tara's? More importantly, did you notice the correct usage of grammar and spelling?

Well there you go. This is just another trolling account. But don't worry your

pretty little asses, Hayley was real.

I did rather well, considering this was my first trolling attempt (I'm thirteen). I covered my track well. Who's going to figure out my real accounts? Only two people, other than myself, know that I'm trolling. A surprising ammount of people expressed that I am (was) Tara Gilesbie. I had expected nobody to fall for it, you see.

Anyway, it started when I made a fake myspace. That continued on toa fake facebook, where I met dear Hayley. Then came the fake fanfiction account made with "Tara's" new "friend" Hayley. You've been such a help, love, without you I might never have made this "story".

But there were some people who were mean to "Tara". I know she's an uber-retard (to quote Hayley), but why should you all be so mean to her? I decided that for Raven's facebook I wuold announce that Tara had to go to the hopital again because she slit her wrists. I believe that some people had applauded the fact that Tara might die. I don't think you truly hated her. So the lesson here is be nice to super tards that can't write for shit.

Oh... And guess what? I'm not a "goff". Or a poser. Or a prep! Just sayin'.

I don't think I'll delete this account. I imagine that my reader's reviews are going to be rather fascinating.

Thus concludes my fantastic trolling attempt that could have gone wonderfully well, had Hayley not stepped into the picture. I still don't blame you dear, this was such fun.

Peace, love, and tacos to you all. :)

Chapter 14.

(AN OK GUISE DI IS 4 U!1111- HALY)(I know it probably won't have the same effect now though)

I wok up frm my dreem, I DREMD I wos clevor an it scarred muh. Hairy wos slepping beside muh and suldenly I wus rly horneh so I woke him up,

Harry babeh I sed sexily

Wut he sed sleepily.

I wisperd 2 him den we had sex, I felt so gud!11 he stuk his wand in muh hole and we did it passionutly.

Sudanly I herd a noise dat sunded lik whispering, I was scred, draco came,

Hi darko I sed

Hi he sed back

Then he kissed meuh

OMFG Leev me alone u sicko I sed running out da tent.I went further in2 tha forest and I came acros a unicorn man. Da unicorn man jamped on yup of me

Leve me alone I sed He didn't RAP!1111 RAP!111111 I cryd

Den came draco, ADVA KEBABRA!1 He cried

He had suvd muh lire and now da unicrn man wus ded

He tuk me bak 2 da tent

Moon wus sad Ginana I had a weird dreem she sed

Omg me 2 I sed , she bagn 2 explan and den I realizd........ OUR DREEMS WER DA SAM!11

Chapter 15.

(An// Hayley, dear, I hadn't expected you to continue this. I don't complain, though. This might be fun. I think I might rape English in this chapter... Just to see what it's like. PREPZ NO FLAMIN)

gianna i dreemed that i hat intiligins i sed 2 my frend.

omfg me 2 she sed.

havin smartiklz waz fun i sed.

yea gianna sed bak 2 me so thin she sed how abut tmrw we go an git sum crak an cokain *(AN// Because, according to the original Tara, crack and coke are completely different thing)* an may b if we git hi den we wil hav dat sam dreem agen.

ok sounz gud i sed.

so den i had sum sex wif drako an i had a rly gud tim. cuz i gut an organism!!!!!!!!!!!!!!!!!!!!!!!!!!!!!!!!!!!11111111111111111111111111

den wen we wok up in da murnin i put on a wite mesh skirt wif sparlkz an mi shit waz a pink wif pees sines and hartz and faryz an raynboz and unicurnz an musik notz an smily fases an resycl sines al ovr it. Mi shuz wer pink converz. *(AN// Tara , where ever she may be, is shouting at the rest of her friends about what a prep I am being.)*

hey u luk rly sexy sed drako

u 2 i sed bak cu it wuz tru.

den giana cam ovr wif da crak an cok. hi letz smok da drugz now i sed.

ok she sed.

so den we smokd it an it wuz rly kul cuz it felt fabluz.
sudnly.................................. giana sprutd an xtra hed!!!!!!!!!!!!!!!!!!!!!!!!!11111111111111111

OMFG i yeld cuz it wuz rly werd.

den i srtatd runin arund cuz it wuz so werd dat giana hadd 2 heds now.

sudnely i ran in2 a tree. *(AN// Tell me this doesn't make you laugh. Oh, erm, it doesn't? Never mind, then.)*

sun i wok up in da hospitl of hogwutz. my fas wuz al covrd in bandajz cuz wenevr i rn in2 da tree i hit mi fas on it.

ow i sed.

hi sed a voyc. it waz...j k rowlin!!!11111111111111111111111

(AN// Poor English language. I wish I hadn't raped you. I won't do it again, I promise. Oh, and remember when Draco tells Moon he's a vampire, but he says Ebony? lolz. I did that on purpose, just sayin.)

Chapter 16.

Just wondering...

Do you want MOAR CHAPTERZ???

Review, bitches.

If you don't review, you're a stupid poser prep and I hope you die.

Chapter 17.

(AN// Aw, you guys want more. I'm touched. By the way, this is Georgia, who is not Hayley. Thought you ought to know my name. Oh, and if you flame I wont

insist that you're a prep, but instead tell you that you suck balls. By the way, my
fucked up mind came up with some pretty crazy shit this chapter. But I felt that
J. K. Rowling needed an interesting death.)

"lol" i sed2 j k roling. "ur story iz ok, but sinse ur not goffik i hav2 kill u
now, lol"

"w8!!!!" sed giana *(AN// I refuse to explain how she showed up.)* "may b we
can mak her goffik2!!!" she sed.

"lol ok"

so we gave j k rowling sum goffik clothz. she wor a blak dres wit strapz
an purpl korset stuf on it and da botum waz al frily and it had purpl on
it2. he shuz wer blak butz wit silvr buklz and rly big platfurmz. she had a
blak skul braslet wit beedz an a pare of eerinz wit blak an gray strz on
dem. she had red i shado an blak i linr dat waz runnin al down her fase.
she also had blak listik an wit fondatun. den we died *(geddit cuz wer
goffik)* her hare blak wit pink strekz in it.

"wtf moon. i cud hav just dun da goffikus spell." sed giana.

"stfu." i replid.

den loopin cam in!!!!!111 he had hiz hand don hiz pantz!!!!!!!!!!!!11111
he luked at j k rolin. den he puled out a gun an shot her!!!!!!!

"omfg!!!!!!!!!!11111111111111111111111111" yeled me an giana. den
loopin srtated2 rape her!!!!!!!!!!

"wtf" i sed. den me and gianna ran away cuz we arr returrded self
insertun marysuez an we didnt kno wut else2 do. den i had buttsecks
wit draco wile giana had buttseks wit hary.

*(AN// Sorry. Just ignore all that crazy shit there. And if you don't review, the
BAMF of Hogwarts (Neville Longbottom) is going to feed your penis to Snape.)*

THE END

Bonus Story 1. I'm Not Okay

Fifteen-year-old Eternity Demen'tia Johnson warily took a seat on the Hogwarts Express. As she did so, she heard many giggles in the air. Ugh. Stupid preps. Eternity had hoped she wouldn't see any when she came to Hogwarts. They had made her life in Los Angeles High School miserable. Now she was supposed to put up with them here? She sighed sadly, and stared out of the window. In her misery, she took her iPod out of her Emily the Strange bag and blared on some My Chemical Romance (A/N: Don't they rock?). Oh great. Now even *more* preps were giving her dirty looks. Eternity tried her best to ignore them. It wasn't because Eternity was dirty or deformed or anything. Maybe it was something to do with her black leather corset, or her ripped black miniskirt or her black combat boots or the metal music she was listening to. Eternity hated how people judged her like that just because she was a goth.

She was beautiful, with long raven black hair with red streaks, deathly pale ivory skin and piercing blue eyes that would make any goth man's heart beat like a subway train. She was skinny, but had curves in the right places. But her eyes still bore the sadness of the scars of her tragic past.

When she was two, Eternity's parents (she was a pureblood) had committed suicide by slitting their wrists. She was adopted when she was five, but all was not well. Her new life was hell. She was constantly abused, beat and raped by her new adopted parents. Every night, she would sit down and cry in her bed. Even at school, she was always being bullied. Her life was totally fucked-up and she couldn't stand it. When she was eleven, she kept getting mail and stuff from Hogwarts but her adopted parents wouldn't let her go. Finally, at fourteen, she was forced to run away.

Anyway, Eternity saw someone trying to sit down next to her. She jumped to her feet.

"Get the fuck out of here you fucking bastard!" she shouted.

"What's wrong?" asked the person. Suddenly Eternity felt calmed down. The person had a very low, sexy voice.

"Oh, I'm sorry!" Eternity apologized.

"It's all right. Now can I at least fucking sit here?" asked the boy.

"Fine." said Eternity.

They boy sat down. Eternity looked at his face. He was extremely hot. He had long dyed black hair and blue eyes.

"What's you're name?" asked Eternity.

"Draco." he said.

"That's an unusual name. But I guess I can't fucking talk. My name's Eternity." said Eternity.

"Cool." said Draco. Eternity and Draco shook hands.

"How old are you?" Eternity wanted to know.

"Fifteen. How about you?" asked Draco.

"Same."

Then, the train stopped and Draco and Eternity had to separate.

THE END

Bonus Story 2. Ghost of You

Chapter 1. Helena

a/n: the other story got a bit boring so here goes and if you're one of the fuckers who flamed Tara's story u can go 2 hell, cause she helped with this. I don't give a fuck when HP takes place. This takes place NOW, and it's MY story, so they can have iPods and NORMAL clothes and shit if I want them 2. So if you're against goths or a prep or something then do everyone a favor and fuck off.

Hermoine Granger checked her black lipstick in her black makeup mirror as she trudged her way to the Hogwarts Express. Last year, she probably would have seen a freak with a bushy mass of hair and brown eyes.

But after the events of this summer, she certainly didn't. Hermione had changed over the summer. Her parents had revealed to her during their summer vacation in America that they were not in fact her parents at all, rather, both her parents were wizards- and she had been adopted by the Grangers- the Grangers, who had spat on her, abused her, neglected her for so long *(Note: And yes, this is possible because it is never implied that it's NOT true.)* The nights Hermoine had spent suffering in her room, whishing it would all stop...They refused to reveal to her who her parents were and why she had been abandoned. In her rage, Hermione- or Maya, as she was now called- had murdered them, using magic. This was unknown to the Ministry. Hermione spent the rest of the summer in Tokyo at Cho's apartment with her and Ginny. She had grown very close to both of them.

Now as she embarked the train to her sixth year, Maya swished her

nearly waist-length, newly dyed raven locks and blinked her emerald- with the use of magic- eyes as she stepped into a seat on the Hogwarts Express. She wore a black leather bustier, a blue plaid mini trimmed with black lace, ripped black fishnets and black lace-up platform boots. On her face was lots and lots of black eyeliner, blood-red lipstick, and matching eyeshadow. Her skin was pale white from the lack of sunlight, and she was slender, but with curves in all the right places. She took out her iPod and put on an Evanescence song at full volume. Some preps stared at her.

"Oh my like god, what are you, like, listening to?" gasped Luna, who was sitting on another seat with a bunch of giggly blonde preps wearing a pink mini, a slutty pink halter top and Gucci shoes. She looked exactly like Hilary Duff. Some preps next to her giggled. Maya stuck up her white-skinned middle finger at them. They gasped. Hermoine went back to listening to her iPod. She changed the song to an My Chemical Romance one and tried to drown out the prep's voices by listening to Gerard's incredible, sexy voice and thinking about him. Suddenly, someone tapped her on the shoulder.

"Fuck!" she screamed. She looked behind her. Virginia *(there's u Tara luvya gurl lolz!)* and Cho, whose nickname is Dementia after her middle name, (Filly u rock bitch, MCR rock 666!1) were standing next to her, looking excited. Ginny was wearing a sexy black corset dress with red lacing, pink fishnets and black high heeled boots. She was wearing black lipstick and eyeliner and her hair was dyed blood-red, with black tips. Dementia had new purple streaks in long, silky ebony hair and was wearing a torn black MCR t-shirt, a ripped black and red plaid mini, safety pin earrings and black combat boots with heels.

"Well, that's nice." said Dementia.

"Oh, sorry. Sit down, my bitches." Maya said jokingly.

Her friends trooped in and sat next to her. Maya noticed now who she was sitting behind- Draco Malfoy. As he heard her voice, he looked around coyly for a split-second and then looked back. His hair was dyed black and slicked back (a/n: kinda like Tom Felton in the first movie). His eyes were icy blue and suggested inner depths of darkness.

Maya and the girls high-fived and chatted for a while. After some time, Ginny asked, "So have you seen the guys?"

"You mean Harry and Ron? No." said Maya.

"Well, you better find them soon because they're gonna be lovin' your new look." said Dementia.

Just then, the train stopped. The girls got out, grinning, freaking out preps. Maya didn't see Harry or Ron, but she just might have seen a boy in leather pants, a leather jacket, black hair and blue eyes smile at her.

Chapter 2. The Beautiful People

a/n: if ur a prep, DON'T READ THIS STORY. If you're not please help me out by suggesting some goth bands and movies for me to reference. Thanx.

After the train ride Eternity and the other students got off the train. Eternity was shocked. In front of her was a beautiful castle. A very tall bearded man asked them to follow him into little boats. Draco waved good-bye to Eternity and made death's touch sign *(a/n: if u don't know what that is I suggest u fuck off to a Britney Spears concert or something)*. Eternity and the others trooped inside the big castle.

"Is this the school?" she asked a fourth-year next to her.

"Yeah." said the fourth-year.

"It's beautiful." said Eternity.

"You think that's beautiful?" a preppy first-year girl with blonde hair wearing a Hilary Duff t-shirt asked.

"Why the fuck not?" Eternity asked defensively.

"Yuck, it looks scary to me." said the girl and Eternity rolled her eyes.

"Ignore her. She's just another stuck-up prep." said another girl next to Eternity. Eternity looked at the girl. She was pretty and looked about fifteen and she had long black hair with purple streaks up to her waist and one forest-green eye and one blue one. She was wearing a long flowing black dress under her school uniform and fishnets and combat boots underneath that.

"What's your name?" Eternity asked her.

"Fillipa *(a/n: Filly there's a shout-out 2 u girlfriend!)* Clarke. Call me Filly if you want. But my middle name's Shadow. You could call me that too." she said. They shook hands.

Then they had to separate because Eternity had to follow Hagrid and the first-years into a magnificent hall. Banners were draped everywhere and four long tables were in the room.

An old man with a long beard introduced himself.

"I am Professor Dumbledore. Welcome back." he said. He made a long speech then he brought out an old wrinkly hat to sort them into houses.

"Let the sorting begin!" he announced.

Eternity gasped then, because the hat burst into song. After he sang the song, everyone clapped. The sound of applause filled the large room. Some people went down to be sorted. When it was Eternity's turn, she sat down nervously on the wooden chair and her heart beat like thunder.

"Slytherin!" shouted the hat. Happiness filled Eternity. How could it be? Draco looked at her his grey-blue eyes filled with joy. Eternity shrugged and sat down at the Slytherin table next to Shadow.

The night went on and Hogwarts had a feast. Meanwhile Shadow introduced Eternity to her friends. (Draco was one of them.) She pointed to a girl with long purple hair with black tips wearing ripped jeans and an Atreyu t-shirt *(a/n: that's u, Tara!)*.

"That's Elvira." she said. Then she introduced Eternity to another boy with black hair and green eyes.

"Hey, bitch." grinned Elvira.

"And that's Darren. He's a half-vampire." she said pointing to the boy.

"Hi." said Darren.

The four of them talked about Marilyn Manson and the Underworld movies for a while and made fun of Christina Aguilera and Hilary Duff. Then, it was time to go to the dormitories.

Chapter 3. Duality

a/n: look, I don't care when the f Harry Potter is in my version it takes place now. BTW, please come up with some goth books and movies. If u notice I used some of the gothic bands! PS: NO PREPS.

After dinner Eternity had to get back into a line with the first-years (she was part of them but much older) and Draco and another girl lead them upstairs into the Slytherin dorm. *(a/n: in this story Draco and Pansy r cousins.)* Eternity got to go to the front of the line to talk to Draco. She plunged her booted feet onto the stone floor and did so until she was at the front of the line. The other girl talking to Draco was had long ebony locks with blue streaks in them. She wore lots of white foundation and black eyeliner. She looked just like the girl in Linkin Park's video for *Crawling*. *(a/n: Eternity looks more like Amy Lee.)*

"What's your name?" Eternity asked her.

"I'm Pansy Parkinson. Well, that's what my motherfucking parents called me. Call me Sea." she replied.

"And I'm Eternity." said Eternity.

Draco just smiled shyly at Eternity through his silvery-blue eyes and black hair.

They walked upstairs to the dorms. Eternity couldn't help noticing that the castle looked a lot like the one in Dracula. As she, Draco, Sea and

the first-years went up the staircases, a lot of preps from other houses stared at them looking scared. A girl with brown hair and brown eyes kept staring at them. She was talking (probably about cheerleading or some shit like that) with a girl with long blonde hair. Eternity stuck her middle finger up at the girls. The girls gasped, their eyes got big, and they turned around.

"Who the hell were they?" Eternity asked Draco.

"Hermione Granger. The girl next to her was Luna Lovegood." said Draco.

"They're such goddamn bitches." said Sea.

"And the biggest fucking preps ever." added Draco.

Eternity couldn't help but agree.

They stopped at a portrait. It was of a girl with pale skin, long black hair and black nails. She was the splitting image of the lead singer of Sisters of Mercy.

"What the fuck? Why aren't we at the door?" asked Eternity.

"You'll see." said Sea.

"Password?" asked the girl.

"*Bleeding kisses*." Draco said to the girl.

"Correct." said the girl and the portrait swung back to reveal a hole.

The first years, Draco and Sea stepped inside. Eternity did too.

Suddenly, she was face-to-face with Gerard Way.

"Oh my fucking god! I so fucking love your band!" she screamed.

"Huh?" asked Gerard.

"Hold on, hold on. That's not Gerard." laughed Elvira.

"That's Satan. Everyone says he looks like Gerard." said Shadow.

"Not that that's a bad thing!" said Darren.

"Dude, I *love* MCR." said Satan laughingly. Eternity smiled and they shook their pallid hands.

Satan had long black hair up to his chin, just like Gerard. His eyes were pale blue and misty, like tears Eternity cried every night. He wore black eyeliner and black nail polish.

"Do you happen to like Slipknot or Sisters of Mercy?" asked Eternity in a flirty voice.

"They kick ass!" agreed Satan. He and Eternity immediately began talking.

The night went on really well. Eternity and her new friends talked about bands like Slipknot, MCR, Evanescence, GC, Marilyn Manson, Sisters of Mercy, Bauhaus, Dead Can Dance, Christian Death, Joy Division, The Cure, Siouxsie and the Banshees, Clan of Xymox, Fields of the Nephilim, Southern Death Cult, 45 Grave, X-mal Deutschland, Garden of Delight.

They all agreed that they rocked and they all hated shitty pop bands like BSB and Play. They used razors to slit their wrists when they felt depressed. The crimson regret flowed out on their pale white skin. They gave each other makeovers with black eyeliner, white foundation and lipstick and they read Dracula and Point Horror books out loud to each other with all the lights turned out and only flashlights.

Eternity felt overjoyed. Just a week ago she had been the only person in her school who had dyed black hair or black eyeliner instead of lip gloss and blonde hair, liked Slipknot or Linkin Park or MCR rather than Hilary Duff or Destiny's Child, slit her wrists, thought about suicide, wore black, shopped at Hot Topic rather than Limited Too, swore, liked rock or was depressed. Now there were so many wonderful people just like her. She was ecsastic.

Chapter 4. Bring me to Life

Eternity woke up the next morning. She brushed her teeth, combed her hair, and then went to her closet. She put on a long black dress that was all ripped and torn, with pink stuff underneath (kind of like the one Amy Lee wore to the Grammies) and then put on big black combat boots.

Shadow, Elvira and Sea all got up and

"You are *so* lucky, bitch." moaned Shadow while she put on her own clothes (a long black dress with a corset at the top, pointy high-heeled boots, and fishnets).

"You have such a great body." added Sea, putting on a ripped black dress with no sleeves that looked exactly like the one the lead singer of her favorite goth band had worn to the MTV Awards that year. (Elvira put on a long black velvet dress with crimson lace.)

Eternity laughed but secretly she knew what her friends meant. They were all skinny, but not as much as her, and they all only had size-B bras. She sadly put her hair up in a messy half-bun, (kind of like Amy Lee has in the video for 'Going Under'.) put on tons of eyeliner and black lipstick, and went downstairs with her friends.

At the breakfast table, she ate Count Chocula cereal and drank red wine even though it was only breakfast. Darren had made a request for human blood, so he drank that and let his friends try some. (Eternity loved it.) They all clinked their glasses.

"To depression." said Eternity.

"To darkness." said Satan.

"To vampires." said Sea.

"To heavy metal music." said Shadow.

"To Eternity." said Draco.

Everyone started giggling, except for Draco. Eternity's pale complexion turned red.

Everyone went off to their classes. Eternity hated all of the classes, even though she was good at them. In Transfiguration class, Eternity had to sit next to a bunch of gigging blonde girls. Their teacher, Professor McGonagall made a speech, and then made them practice transfiguration on a bunch of ants they would try to turn into pencils.

Everyone was trying, but it didn't work for them. Suddenly, Eternity found herself pointing to the ant and saying a spell...

Suddenly, the ant turned into a gigantic black unicorn with huge black wings and flew out the window.

Everyone in the room gasped.

Later, Professor McGonagall had a talk with Eternity.

"Eternity, you are being moved up to your fifth year." she said.

Chapter 5. In the Shadows

a/n: TARA IS DA BIGGEST FUCKING BITCH EVER AND BY THE WAY I'M A BIGGER MCR FAN AND GERARD IS MINE 4EVA SO FUCK U! AND I'M NOT GIVING U UR SWEATER BACK!

Eternity was so happy. She went to class with the other fifth-years, Sea, Draco, Shadow, Darren and Satan. That fucking retard Elvira (whose real name was Lindsay like that fucking ho Lindsay Loan) had gone all the way back to first-year and they put her in Gryffindor where all the retarded preps were because she couldn't even write properly and she had to get her friends 2 do it for her.

Anyway, Eternity woke up from her dark slumber and got ready for the coming day, which she hated so much. She put on a black leather minidress with black fishnets and black pointy boots. She put some blue streaks in her shower of flowing black raven locks. Then she put on some mascara, white foundation, black lipstick, and eyeliner. Allt the gothic bois starred at her, their piercing blue eyes getting wide. The preps did too but for a different reason. She put up your middle finger at them. Then anyway she put on sum MCR music. She plunged her black feet into the stone cold ground and walked to Transfiguration.

"Hello everyone." said Proffesor McGonagal staring at them out of her giant eyes. "You will all be doing something different this time. You will all have partners." She made everyone find a partner. Eternity's partner was.... Draco!

THE END

MY IMMORTAL CHARACTER RELATIONSHIP DIAGRAM/CHART THING

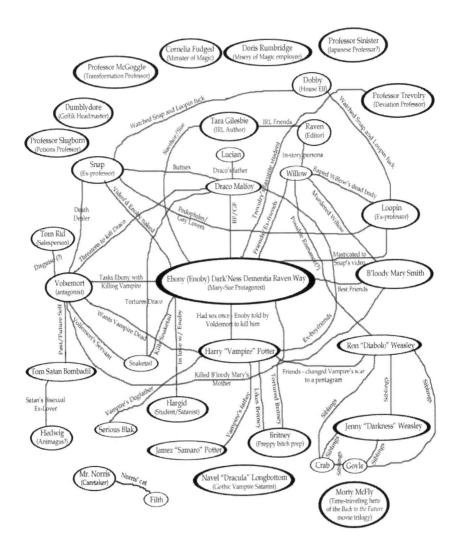

Additional Notes

* **Bloody Gothic Rose 666** - Gothic Metal band composed of Enoby, B'loody Mary, Draco, Vampire, Diabolo, and Hargid
* **XBlakXTearX** - Gothic Metal band composed of Lucian, Snap, Samaro, and Serious

EBONY
DARK'NESS
DEMENTIA
RAVEN
WAY

My Immortal is the most famous, notoriously bad fan fiction ever written. Based *very* loosely in the *Harry Potter* universe and featuring the blatant Mary-Sue protagonist Ebony (or often times "Enoby"), it reads like a detailed list of everything a fanfic author could ever possibly do wrong, only taken to exaggerated, horrifying extremes.

Written by super-tard **Tara Gilesbie aka. XXXbloodyrists666XXX**, *My Immortal* was originally posted to fanfiction.net sometime in 2006, but was subsequently deleted by the ff.net staff after causing a severe drop in the site's collective IQ. In fact, the fanfic is so unbelievably bad that many refuse to accept that it's real, insisting that Tara was only trolling and that the story is really a parody.

Regardless of the author's intent, *My Immortal* remains one of the most cringeworthy, unintentionally hilarious, so-bad-it's-good pieces of literature the internets have ever shat out and is one of the most famous writings of the ~~20th~~ LOL RETARDED 21st century equivalent to such authors as Emily Dickinson, F. Scott Fitzgerald, and John Steinbeck.

This definitive collection also includes the unofficial sequel *My Immortal 2: Wake Me Up Inside*, the official sequels *My Immortal 2: Fangz 4 De Venom* and *A Vampre Wil Nevr Hurt You*, co-authored with **Xanthan Gum** as well as the smash hit spin-offs *I'm Not Okay* and *Ghost of you* by **Bloodytearz666**. Also included is a guest appearance of **Obvious Troll**.

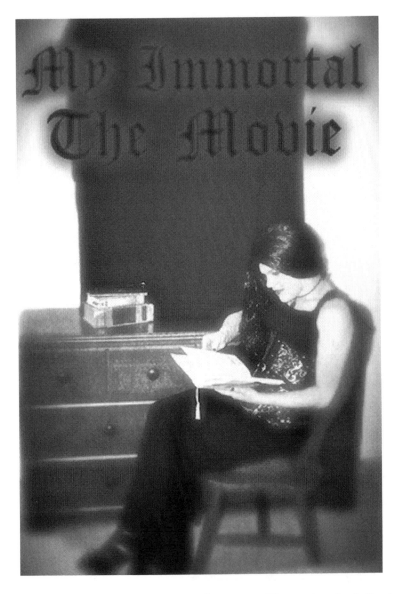

Don't forget to check out America's most goffik movie adaptation!
Featuring *My Immortal: The Movie*!
http://lucky13productions.net/

Made in the USA
Middletown, DE
14 March 2019